# THE ONE MAN'S MAN'S FAMILY ALBUM

Mollie Lee Pryor

I say Carlton thanks most awfully for being my American foster-parent
Pat.

Always "Bark"

**Preceding page** *(left to right)* Page Gilman, Michael Raffetto, Kathleen Wilson, J. Anthony Smythe, Winifred Wolfe, Bernice Berwin, Minetta Ellen, Walter Patterson and Barton Yarborough. (1932)

# THE ONE MAN'S FAMILY ALBUM

**An inside look at radio's
longest running show**

## Seven Stones Press

Woodside    •    California

**ISBN 0-940249-05-7**

Cover and book design by David Charlsen
Cover photograph hand-colored by Barbara Wyeth

All photographs, unless otherwise noted, are from the collection of
Carlton E. Morse. We have attempted to trace the ownership of all
copyrighted material in the picture sections, as well as to contact all
persons portrayed. The publisher regrets any inadvertent error, and
will be happy to make necessary corrections in any future printings.
The bound manuscripts from the *Carlton E. Morse Collection* are
located at Stanford University.
Carlton E. Morse   (M362)
Department of Special Collections and University Archives
Stanford University Libraries

For additional copies of this book check your local bookstore, or you
may write directly to the publisher:

**Seven Stones Press**
Star Route   Box 50
Woodside, CA 94062

Please enclose $8.95 for each book, plus $1.50 per book for shipping
and handling. California residents please add appropriate sales tax.

For a complete listing of Seven Stones Press publications, please see
the last page of this book.

*Dedicated to*

*Michael Raffetto*

*Bernice Berwin*

*and Page Gilman*

# Acknowledgements

I would like to pay tribute to Dr. Walter Sheppard for his research and thesis that culminated in his 506-page volume *One Man's Family: A History and Analysis*. I have been both confounded and delighted at his vast assemblage of facts and figures. His effort has great depth and breadth and at the same time never loses the flavor and spirit of the family saga. For me, above all, it offers the fascination of being able to relive those 27 good years, with all my vivid memories aroused and brought into focus by Dr. Sheppard's careful survey.

# Contents

# Foreword

When I was very young, I used to spend long hours sitting on the rug in front of the Philco console radio that dominated the far end of our living room. That radio was my magic carpet. It took me places I had never dreamed of.

Often I would sit there alone, entranced. But you could bet that when it came time for "One Man's Family," my family would be sitting there in the living room with me, like millions of other Americans. The Barbour family was the best-known and best-loved family in the United States from 1932 to 1960. Since my entire family consisted of only my mother, father, brother and one aunt, the Barbours became, in a sense, our electronic relatives.

It seems strange now, looking back on it, that we would become so attached to those voices that entered our lives through the loudspeaker of our radio. Perhaps one reason was, we didn't know the names of the actors, only their mysterious creator—Carlton E. Morse. I wasn't listening to the actor Michael Raffetto; I was hearing Paul Barbour. Hazel wasn't actress Bernice Berwin, she *was* Hazel, as real to me as my Aunt Dot.

A few years ago, when I finally met Mike Raffetto and Bernice Berwin, it was difficult to accept them as anyone but Paul and Hazel. Such was the hold the Barbours of Sea Cliff had on my imagination.

In today's hectic world of electronic wonders, where programs and people come and go in a flash, it's almost impossible to understand that kind of listener loyalty. But it happened to me. Later I learned that same kind of bonding happened to millions of other people: mental pictures indelibly printed on the minds of the radio generation.

In 1985, something I could never have dreamed of, happened. I was asked to create a program honoring Carlton E. Morse; bits and pieces from his old radio shows woven into the story of a master storyteller's life. What a thrill! I began to research the life of that shy, bespectacled ex-newspaperman who became the patron saint of the American family. It was a labor of love, for it was Carlton's broadcasts that charted the course of the rest of my life. He was the reason I went into radio, and the genesis of what has turned out to be a wonderful career in broadcasting.

Working on the tribute to Carlton, I listened to endless hours of "One Man's Family" broadcasts. Sometimes, tampering with memories results in disappointment. But as I listened to those old radio shows, I realized they were, if anything, even better than I had remembered. The dialogue was superb, the acting outstanding and the production techniques first-rate. This shouldn't have been surprising. After all, Carlton and his cast invented radio acting.

Oh, there were actors on radio before "One Man's Family," but they were stage actors who still projected to the top balcony as they stood in front of the microphone. The effect was ludicrous, but it was the accepted style. Carlton would have none of it. He wanted his actors to talk the way his listeners talked in real life.

After the first few shows were broadcast transcontinentally out of San Francisco, New York issued the following order to its upstart producer: "Have your actors speak louder. Talk up!" Carlton's feisty reply: "This is normal voice quality, and that is what people in this situation would do. Your engineers are simply going to have to live with it."

Since The Family was such a success by that time, New York allowed the talented tail to wag the executive dog. Within a year, there were half-a-dozen dramatic shows on the air in which the dialogue was performed with a sense of naturalness, not stage techniques.

Now, Carlton has put a number of scripts into book form for all of us who listened to, and loved, "One Man's Family." It's been quite a job. Imagine trying to select from 3,256 episodes those special moments that capture the essence of 28 years dedicated to "the mothers and fathers of the younger generation, and their bewildering offspring."

For me, and I hope for you, this book will be the ultimate family reunion thanks to the Boswell of the American family—Carlton E. Morse.

**Dave McElhatton**
Senior News Anchor—KPIX
San Francisco—April, 1988

# CHAPTER ONE

# The Way It Was!

On Tuesday, April 12, 1932, a cool, foggy day in San Francisco, a cast of nine veteran radio actors, an announcer, a sound man and Carlton E. Morse gathered at four o'clock in Studio B of the National Broadcasting Company's West Coast headquarters at 111 Sutter Street in San Francisco. This was the first reading rehearsal for *Chapter One, Book One* of "One Man's Family" which began:

> "Announcer: One Man's Family is dedicated to the Mothers and Fathers of the younger generation, and to their bewildering offspring".

The original theme was *Destiny Waltz,* played by Paul Carson. Later, Carson composed a theme especially for the show which he called *Valse Patricia.*

Months earlier Morse had submitted the first three episodes of "One Man's Family" to NBC. The heads of the West Coast production department had turned thumbs down. Both the Program Manager and the Production Director shook their heads lugubriously and said *"NO".* They got Morse into the Program Manager's Office and said, quite frankly: "Morse, this 'One Man's Family' tripe is pure tripe! Morse, you are written out! Morse, you lack imagination! Everybody *lives* a family life, day in and day out! Year in, year out! Who wants to turn on his radio and listen to *more* family life?"

You must admit this was discouraging, but Morse didn't believe them. He was steeped in John Galsworthy's *The Forsyte Saga,* and knew such a popular book demonstrated that a family story could be popular on radio, too. He finally took his three episodes of "One Man's Family" to NBC West Coast Vice President, Don E. Gilman, who kept the scripts for about three weeks. Finally, he called Morse into the front office and said "I like this family idea

The Original Cast and Creator: *(from left to right)* Page Gillman, Minetta Ellen, Walter Patterson, Bernice Berwin, Mrs. Carlton E. (Patricia) Morse, Carlton E. Morse, Kathleen Wilson, Barton Yarborough, Winifred Wolfe, and J. Anthony Smythe. (1932)

very much, but I'm not sure the radio listening audience will hold still for it. Now then, if we put this on the air, will you write the episodes so that we can bring the show to an end after six weeks if it doesn't catch on?"

Morse promised. Well, the first episode went on the air at 9:30 p.m., Friday, April 29, 1932, and it was never off the air until the show closed over 27 years later. In fact, it had one sponsor, *Standard Brands,* for 17 of those years.

Morse tells the following story:

> *"Chapter One, Book One* originally was scheduled for presentation on Station KPO and the Pacific Coast Network on Wednesday, April 13. I do not remember what happened, but this beginning episode entitled 'Introduction of the Barbour Family' did not make its appearance until Friday, April 29, and was rescheduled for the half hour from 9:30 to 10:00 in the evening."

In the introductory lines explaining this original show, Morse said:

"This is neither an expose of youth's foibles, nor an accusation against the older generations, but merely a cross-section of the life of a modern family [vintage 1932], given with the hope of explaining father to son and son to father. Controversial subjects are dealt with from each individual character's point of view, and have no ulterior motive save to explain certain given types of personalities who have developed in recent years. Every mother and father with a growing family has, in 1932, problems no other parents in history have had to face."

The original cast of "One Man's Family" was selected from actors Morse had come to know as writer and director at NBC where he as on the staff. He had been engaged in writing mystery and adventure serials, a reinterpretation of classic myths for radio, a western historical series and numerous other writing chores at NBC since 1929. From these actors Morse chose:

| | |
|---|---|
| J. Anthony Smythe | *Father Henry Barbour* |
| Minetta Ellen | *Mother Fanny Barbour* |
| Michael Raffetto | *Paul Barbour* |
| Bernice Berwin | *Hazel Barbour* |
| Barton Yarborough | *Clifford Barbour* |
| Kathleen Wilson | *Claudia Barbour* |
| Page Gilman | *Jack Barbour* |

The Barbours were very much a reflection of the American people and their times. "One Man's Family" struck an emotional nerve for hundreds of thousands who were suffering from the economic crisis and widespread unemployment resulting from the crash of '29. It was a bold stroke to cast Father Barbour as the president of a bond house at a time when bond salesmen were not held in high regard. At first, Father Barbour was not an entirely sympathetic character. He was set in his ways; his integrity could be almost daunting. But as he developed he was clearly a man of substance, blessed with strength and solid knowledge.

Mother Barbour epitomized the traditional womanly virtues. She accepted her role of housewife and child-rearer gracefully and was supremely loyal to her husband. Morse described her as "a staunch weather vane in a stormy climate, pointing always to the eventual triumph of fair weather".

Paul, their eldest son and the designated heartthrob of the program, was a veteran of World War I. A pilot in France, he had married an American Army nurse only to lose her during a hospital epidemic even before the show began. Thereafter he was a confirmed bachelor, but Morse introduced several girlfriends. Paul adopted a daughter, Teddy, a few years into the show and she became a beloved member of the Barbour family.

Hazel, the eldest daughter, married twice during the course of the show and produced three children. Her character was portrayed as a serene gentle young mother.

The twins, Clifford and Claudia, were always the tempestuous members of the brood—perhaps the reason so many listeners identified with them. Claudia ran the gamut of emotional experiences from hilarious and slightly ribald comedy to deeply passionate love scenes and unrestrained misery.

The youngest cast member and Carlton E. Morse discuss a scene.

She eloped with Johnny Roberts while in college, but eight months later they quarreled and he disappeared. The next Claudia knew of him, he had been wounded while fighting with the rebels in China. Shortly after he returned home in good health, Johnny was stricken with heart failure and died. From this unfortunate marriage, Claudia received two rewards: a $250,000 fortune and her daughter, Joan. Father Barbour was opposed to Claudia having so much money in her own right, and this disagreement prompted Claudia to take Joan to England. There she met her second husband, Captain Nicholas Lacy, with whom she returned to Sea Cliff and had two more children.

Clifford was a ladies' man, though it seemed they—and life—often rejected him. He eventually married twice, fathered a son, and went to work in his father's securities business.

Jack, the youngest, married only once and with his wife Betty raised six children. He was drafted into the Korean War, and after two years returned from the Pacific to practice law in San Francisco.

For the listening audience, the Barbours were a real family. The "Barbour home" in San Francisco's Sea Cliff district became an attraction for tourists on sightseeing buses (a phenomenon the real owners of the home apparently enjoyed). Listeners wrote get well letters when a member of the family was ill, and sacks full of Christmas cards for the family arrived at NBC every year. A frequent recipient of advice or admonishment was Clifford, who had a knack for getting into scrapes. Numerous babies born to several generations were named after the Barbour children, especially Clifford and Claudia.

At the close of the first reading rehearsal, the reaction of the cast was mixed. Remember, this was the first attempt on radio to create a real, live American family showing down-to-earth human relations between parents and children with an honest attempt at integrity. Morse recalls:

"As I remember, Minetta Ellen (Mother Barbour), Bernice Berwin (Hazel) and Kathleen Wilson (Claudia) were greatly intrigued with the first script. Actually, I don't think any of us saw 27 years of work ahead. I remeber Bart Yarborough (Clifford) slapped his script across his knees after the first reading and said, 'Well, there it is folks, take it or leave it—no bang bangs! Nobody dead, nobody saved in the nick of time! It's either a flop or a sleeper!' Tony Smythe (Father Barbour) was the only one who expressed enthusiasm. As we left the rehearsal studio he slipped his hand under my arm, squeezed and said, 'Carlton, I think you've done it. It's what radio has been waiting to hear.'"

# CHAPTER TWO

## Introducing the Barbours

ANNOUNCEMENTS AND DESCRIPTIONS
FOR
"ONE MAN'S FAMILY"
EPISODE 1

"INTRODUCING THE BARBOUR FAMILY"

**Friday**            **9:30-10:00 p.m.**            **April 29, 1932**

("DESTINY WALTZ")

*ANNOUNCER:* Tonight's episode of "One Man's Family" is entitled "Introducing The Barbour Family."

(ORCHESTRA SWELLS FOR MOMENT...THEN BACKGROUND ANNOUNCER)

*ANN:* "One Man's Family" is dedicated to the Mothers and Fathers of the younger generation and to their bewildering offspring. This is neither an expose of Youth's foibles nor an accusation against the older generation. It is merely a cross-section of the life of a modern family, given with the hope of explaining father to son and son to father. Controversial subjects are dealt with from each individual character's point of view and have no further purpose than to explain certain given types of personalities which have developed in the last few years. Every man with a growing family these days has problems no other father in history has had to face. These 13 episodes deal with the family of Henry Barbour, successful San Francisco stockbroker, who has reached the peak of middle life and is inclined toward contentment with himself and the manner in which he has carried on his life's work. Because you are to become so intimately acquainted with the Barbours in the coming weeks we want you to know them at once. Let me present first, Mrs. Henry Barbour...

*FANNY:* Good evening.

*ANN:* And now Mr. Barbour…

*HENRY:* Good evening…Nice golf weather we're having, isn't it?

*ANN:* Sorry Mr. Barbour, I don't play golf.

*HENRY:* No?…Too bad…Good game.

*ANN:* I'm certain it is…And now Miss Hazel Barbour. Hazel may I tell your age?

*HAZEL:* *(laughs softly)* Why of course.

*ANN:* Thank you…Hazel is the eldest daughter…She is 27…Good looking, too.

*HAZEL:* *(embarrassed laugh)* Why, thank you.

*ANN:* And now I want you to meet the hero of the Barbour family…His name's Paul. Paul is 31, four years older than Hazel. He was an aviator in the World War and was shot down….

(SOUND OF CANE TAPPING)

*ANN:* *(lower voice)* He's coming now…One of Paul's legs was badly injured. He'll use a cane the rest of his life…*(lifts voice)*…Paul, come here and let me introduce you…Folks, this is Lieut. Paul Barbour.

*PAUL:* Oh please…Forget that Lieutenant rubbish, will you…I mean to say, forget EVERYTHING about war.

*ANN:* Why, of course, Paul.

*PAUL:* Thanks.

(SOUND OF CANE RECEDING FROM MIKE)

*ANN:* There are twins in the Barbour family. A girl and a boy; Claudia and Clifford or rather Claud and Cliff. They're just 19. Let me introduce Claudia first.

*CLAUD:* Oh no you don't…Cliff and I go in pairs.

*CLIFF:* Sure, we team up on everything.

*ANN:* *(laughs)* Well then, may I introduce the team of Claud and Cliff.

*CLAUD AND CLIFF:* Cheerio…

*CLAUD:* *(leaving mike)* Got a match Cliff?

*CLIFF:* *(distance)* Sure.

*ANN:* *(laughs)* There's a pair for you…Straight-forward, honest-eyed, loveable… You'll like THEM in spite of yourself…See if you don't…And now just one more member of the family to be accounted for…And really folks, I don't know how to account for him. He really slipped into the family by mistake I think. Anyway here he is. Fourteen-year-old Jack Barbour...

*JACK:* *(politely)* Good evening...*(suddenly)*...Say mister, look at that airplane model...Ain't it a peach...Made it myself...

*ANN:* Wait a minute...Wait a minute, Jack...We'll talk about airplanes another time if you don't mind.

*JACK:* Yes sir...

*ANN:* And so folks, that brings you the Barbour family. Henry Barbour; his wife, Fanny Barbour; Paul, 31; Hazel, 27; Claudia and Clifford, 19; and Jack, 14.

("DESTINY WALTZ")

*ANN:* The story opens in the Barbour's Sea Cliff home, where it stands overlooking the Golden Gate. Mr. and Mrs. Barbour are entertaining Judge Glenn Hunter.

(PAUSE)

*FANNY:* Poke up the fire, Henry...Judge are you comfortable?

*JUDGE:* Perfectly, Mrs. Barbour.

*BARBOUR:* *(leaving mike)* I've got a fireplace complex, I guess, Glenn...*(distance)*...Remember when we were kids, how we used to huddle about the old heater when you came over at our place in the evenings?

*JUDGE:* *(chuckles)* I remember Henry...

*BARBOUR:* *(distance)* Well ever since those days I've sworn I'd have a fireplace... *(pause)* There, that's better.

*FANNY:* He's even got a fireplace in our bedroom.

*BARBOUR:* *(coming to mike)* Yes, I like to sleep looking into the dying embers.

(SOUND OF CANE APPROACHING)

*FANNY:* There's Paul coming in.

*JUDGE:* Fine boy, Paul...How's he doing with his aviation school?...Getting many students?

*BARBOUR:* *(shortly)* A few...

(CANE STOPS)

*PAUL:* *(distance)* Oh sorry...Didn't know you had company.

*FANNY:*   Come on in Paul...It's Judge Hunter.

*JUDGE:*   Hello Paul...How's the boy?

*PAUL:*   *(coming to mike)...(heartily)*...Why hello, Judge...It's been months since you've been out...I mean to say, mighty glad to see you again.

*JUDGE:*   You're looking mighty fine, lad...How's your flying school going?

*FANNY:*   Here, Paul, sit down here beside me.

*PAUL:*   Thanks Mother...Mind if I smoke?

*FANNY:*   *(gently)* If you must Paul...

*PAUL:*   Thanks...Oh, pretty fair, Judge...Guess business is slack everywhere, just now.

*JUDGE:*   Yes, I guess that's about right...

*PAUL:*   *(cynically)* Except in your business...I suppose there are just as many folks able to pay for their crimes as ever.

*JUDGE:*   *(gravely)* I'm afraid that's true, Paul...People seem to have just as much time to devote behind the bars and just as many lives to give on the gallows, as in the most prosperous days.

*BARBOUR:*   *(grunts)* More...The papers don't print ANYTHING but crime anymore...What's the world coming to, Glenn?

*JUDGE:*   *(admits)* In a way that's true, Henry...There is a restlessness...It's the younger generation that's fermenting...

*BARBOUR:*   *(grunts)* The younger generation...It ought to be spanked and sent to bed.

*PAUL:*   *(chuckles)* Like you spank and send to bed Claud and Cliff, eh?

*FANNY:*   *(reprovingly)* Paul!

*BARBOUR:*   *(angrily)* It's just such people as you Paul, who make this unrest...Your half-baked cynicism...Your refusal to take the present structure of social life seriously...Your preference to risking your neck in an old crate of a flying machine teaching youngsters to fly, to coming into a good solid business and taking a partnership with your father.

*FANNY:*   *(gently)* Now Henry...Let's not go over that again...Paul's 31, and it's his privilege to choose his work.

*JUDGE:*   I wouldn't worry Henry...Cliff will soon be out of school and you'll have a mighty fine partner in him.

*BARBOUR:*   That harum-scarum kid!...Why he's one big brainstorm after another...

Glenn, when we were 19 years old we didn't run around, doing as we pleased, did we?

*JUDGE:*   Well now, Henry, it's pretty hard to look back 40 years and tell just what we DID do...It doesn't seem as if we did, though.

*BARBOUR:*   No, of course we didn't...

*JUDGE:*   If you're worrying about your family, Henry, you're doing so needlessly... you've got a mighty fine group of young men and women...You should be proud of them.

*BARBOUR:*   Oh, I'm not WORRYING about them...They wouldn't do anything wrong...It isn't that...It's just things like Paul's aviation business here...Why should any sane young man prefer to spend his life flying around in an airship when he could be amassing a good-sized bank account...Why do Claudia and Clifford keep harping on "freedom"..."more freedom"...Why even Jack—14 years old, mind you—even HE springs wild-eyed sophistry about "personal rights"...I ask you, what is the world coming to?

*FANNY:*   Judge, I'm afraid you've struck Henry's weak spot...

*JUDGE:*   It's an important question in any family-man's life, Mrs. Barbour...In fact, I would say it was the key to the whole turbulent situation in the United States today.

*PAUL:*   It's the first important step in a tremendous social revolution that's taking place in this country...

*BARBOUR:*   *(explodes)* Social revolution...Rot...You and your social revolution.

*JUDGE:*   Henry, I think Paul is nearer the truth than you suspect.

*BARBOUR:*   Revolution means war...

*PAUL: (cynically)* Yes Dad...The sort of war we are participating in this moment...The war of progress with conservatism.

*BARBOUR: (sneers)* I suppose you are trying to get over the idea that it is more progressive to fly a kite than to build a good sound business?

*PAUL:*   No, Dad...But progress is built on unrest...conservatism on self-satisfaction.

*BARBOUR: (stirred up)* Why shouldn't I be satisfied? Haven't I worked hard all my life; haven't I built a business that has put myself and my family in comfortable circumstances for the rest of their lives; haven't I given my children good educations; haven't I taught them the laws of the land and the laws of God? Why shouldn't I gain a little comfort from the fact that I have done my work well?

*FANNY:*   Please, Henry...Don't work yourself up like this...You know you don't sleep well after an argument.

*PAUL:*   Dad, don't misunderstand me...I don't belittle your efforts...I mean to say, I think you've lived splendidly according to your own lights...

*BARBOUR:* Not according to my lights alone...But according to the standards of thinking men throughout the country.

*PAUL:* Yes, men of your generation...A generation that led the world into the most horrible catastrophe known to man...

*JUDGE:* You mean the World War, Paul?

*PAUL:* Yes, Judge...The World War...That's what YOUR generation of thinking men did for the world...And now my generation...Claudia's generation...Jack's generation, have to come along and clean up the mess.

*BARBOUR:* There would be no mess to clean up, if you'd all put your shoulder to the wheel and push together.

*PAUL:* Yes, but where would you have us push?...Right back into the old rut that led to the last war...You'd have us push ourselves into another war.

*BARBOUR:* Nonsense...There'll never be another war...

*PAUL:* *(grimly)* There never will be as far as I'M concerned...Nor as far as Cliff's concerned, nor Jack, if I can help it.

*JUDGE:* *(gravely)* I hope there will not be.

*BARBOUR:* *(bitterly)* Glenn, you don't get the full significance of Paul's words... He means he wouldn't fight if this country were at war.

*FANNY:* Oh, Henry...

*PAUL:* *(grimly)* That's just what I *do* mean...I'd rot in jail before I'd fight again... And I'd rather see Cliff and Jack stood up against a wall and shot, than to be sent into front-line trenches.

*FANNY:* Oh, Paul...

*PAUL:* I mean to say, I'm for this younger generation, heart and soul, no matter what they do...They're going to make this a different sort of country...They're going to make mistakes...lots of them...But they're going to pay for their mistakes gamely and go right on, until they have found out what it's all about and why.

*JUDGE:* *(gravely)* But Paul, unrest leads to war as well as to progress.

*PAUL:* So does the old conservative dog-eat-dog system...That's been proved...We might as well have war ATTEMPTING to progress, as to have it because a few selfish statesmen and financiers can't get along.

(SOUND OF DOOR CLOSING)

*FANNY:* *(calls)* Is that you Hazel?...*(to group)*...She went to the opera...She should be getting in.

(PAUSE)

FANNY:   *(calls)* Hazel, come in...Judge Hunter is here.

(PAUSE)

FANNY:   That's strange...Henry, will you see who it is?

HENRY:   *(leaving mike)* Paul, you must have left the front door ajar, when you came in.

(PAUSE)

JACK:   *(distance)* Oooow...Oooow, Dad, let go my ear...

HENRY:   *(coming to mike)* March right in here to your mother, young man.

JACK:   *(coming to mike)* Oooow, you're hurting my ear...

FANNY:   Why Jack, what are you doing up and dressed?...I sent you to bed at 9:00 and here it is after 11.

JACK:   *(sullen)* Yes ma'am.

HENRY:   *(angrily)* Answer your mother...What were you doing out, when you were told to be in bed?

JACK:   Nothing.

FANNY:   Jack, aren't you going to speak to Judge Hunter?

JACK:   *(sullen)* Good evening, sir.

JUDGE:   Good evening, Jack.

FANNY:   Please, Jack, won't you tell Mother, where you have been?

JACK:   *(sullen)* Out doors.

FANNY:   But where, out doors.

JACK:   Just around places...

FANNY:   Did you go to the theater?

JACK:   No, Mother.

HENRY:   *(exasperated)* Let me take him upstairs...I'll whale it out of him.

FANNY:   Just a moment, Henry...Jack, whom were you with?

JACK:   *(sullen)* A bunch of fellows.

Jack, Father Barbour, and Paul in the library at Sea Cliff.

*FANNY:*   What fellows?...Your Scout troop?

*JACK:*   *(sullen)* No, Mother.

*PAUL:*   I say, old kid.

*JACK:*   *(brightening)* Yes sir?

*PAUL:*   Why don't you 'fess up and take your medicine...That's the only way, you know.

*JACK:*   But I can't Paul...I've promised.

*PAUL:*   I see...It involves someone else, then?

*JACK:*   Yes sir.

*PAUL:*   Well look here...Couldn't you sort of tell it so that you wouldn't poach on anyone else...You see it's Dad and Mother's right to know about you.

*JACK:*   *(hesitates)* Yes sir, I could do that.

*HENRY:*   Nonsense...

*FANNY:*   Please, Henry...Go on Jack.

*JACK:*   Well, us kids has got a sekrit society and they was a speshul meeting on tonight and so everybody had to be there.

*HENRY:*   What sort of secret society?

*JACK:*   Just a sekrit society...

*FANNY:*   And what was this special meeting about?

*JACK:*   Aaaaw...nothing.

*PAUL:*   Special meeting for the election of officers, maybe...Eh Jack?

*JACK:*   No sir...It...*(hesitates)*...It was ladies' night.

*HENRY:*   *(explodes)* WHAT!

(SHOUT OF LAUGHTER FROM JUDGE AND PAUL)

*FANNY:*   Please Paul...This is all very painful...Jack, what do you mean, ladies' night?...Do you mean there were little girls present?

*JACK:*   No ma'am...It was a speshul meeting for everybody what belongs to the club to tell how much they don't like girls...

(MORE LAUGHTER FROM JUDGE AND PAUL)

*HAZEL:* *(distance)* Here...Here...What's all this hilarity about...Am I missing something?

*PAUL:* Come on in Hazel...Sit in on the family inquisition.

*HAZEL:* *(disapproving)* Oh, Jack on the carpet again, eh?...Why good evening, Judge Hunter.

*JUDGE:* My dear, how charming you are...

*HAZEL:* Oh sit still, Judge...I'm afraid you're an old flatterer.

*JUDGE:* Indeed not...Was the opera enjoyable?

*HAZEL:* *(indifferent)* Oh it was alright...

*JACK:* Mother, may I go now?

*HENRY:* You cannot...

*JACK:* *(sullen)* Yes sir...

*FANNY:* So you boys got together to tell how much you disliked girls?

*JACK:* Yes ma'am.

*FANNY:* Was that all?

*JACK:* Then everybody had to swear he wouldn't EVER, EVER have anything to do with them....

*HENRY:* *(sarcastic)* I suppose that includes your mother and sisters.

*JACK:* No sir...Just that we wouldn't go no places with them or nothing.

*HAZEL:* Jack, your English is miserable.

*JACK:* Aaaaw!

*HENRY:* Where did you meet?

(PAUSE)

*FANNY:* Jack, didn't you hear your father speak to you?

*JACK:* Yes ma'am.

*FANNY:* Well, why don't you answer him?

*JACK:* I...*(hesitates)*...It's a sekrit.

*HENRY:* Nonsense...There'll be no secrets in this household as long as I'm at the head of it.

PAUL:   *(lightly)* I hope you don't mean that literally, Dad.

HENRY:   *(angrily)* That's just how I DO mean it, Paul...

PAUL:   Oh I say...

HAZEL:   Dad's absolutely right, Paul.

PAUL:   Well...well...Then supposing you begin, Hazel, by unburdening all the little secrets inside you at the family conference.

FANNY:   Why Hazel, what does he mean?

HAZEL:   I don't know Mother...It's just another one of his hopeless jokes, I suppose.

PAUL:   Nothing of the kind...Do you mean to sit there and say that nothing has ever occurred in your life that isn't a secret from your family?

HAZEL:   How perfectly beastly...Of course there's nothing...

PAUL:   You poor girl...

HENRY:   *(sharply)* That'll be enough of that...Jack, I'll give you until morning to think it over. I want you to come to me before breakfast and tell me where this meeting was held and who was present.

JACK:   *(sullen)* I won't tell.

HENRY:   You will or you'll get the worst whipping you've ever received...Now go to bed, and I hope you'll think better of your decision in the morning.

JACK:   Yes sir...*(pause)*...Father?

HENRY:   Well?

JACK:   Couldn't I have the whipping tonight, sir? I'd sleep better if it was over.

HENRY:   *(angrily)* March up to bed, sir...Do you hear me?

JACK:   Yes sir...*(pause)*...Good night, Judge Hunter.

JUDGE:   Good night, Jack.

(PAUSE)

JACK:   *(distance)* Good night Mother...

FANNY:   Good night, Jack.

(PAUSE)

*HENRY:*   Glenn, what are you going to do with a stubborn child like that?...I know I'll have to whip him in the morning.

*JUDGE:*   Henry, have you ever been able to whip anything out of him?

*HENRY:*   No!

*JUDGE:*   Then why do you continue to whip him?...You admit it does no good.

*HENRY:*   He HAS to be punished.

*JUDGE:*   I thought whipping was to correct, not to punish.

*HENRY:*   Punishment is a method of correction...Certainly as a jurist you should know that.

*JUDGE:*   But you've admitted that it doesn't change the boy...Why don't you look for another method of correction that WILL correct.

*JACK:*   *(coming to mike)* Dad, I'm sorry...

*HENRY:*   I thought I sent you to bed.

*JACK:*   Yes, sir...I just came down to tell you good night...I'm sorry, I went up without saying it.

*HENRY:*   *(embarrassed)* Oh...*(clears throat)*...Why...Why...Good night, Son.

(LONG PAUSE)

*JUDGE:*   *(gently)* You see, Henry...Your sons WANT to be close to you...Why don't you try to understand THEIR viewpoint a little more, instead of always trying to bend them to yours.

*HENRY:*   But the boy's in the wrong...He disobeyed his mother...

*JUDGE:*   You think he told you the truth about what he did tonight, don't you?

*HENRY:*   *(proudly)* Thank God, my children DON'T LIE.

*JUDGE:*   That is something to be mighty proud of, Henry...But why do you suppose Jack sneaked out on you tonight?

*HENRY:*   Because he KNEW I wouldn't consent to his being out this late.

*JUDGE:*   Yes...He knew you wouldn't understand him...You would dismiss his request without a second thought.

*HENRY:*   And that's right...A boy 14 years old has no business out at midnight.

*JUDGE:*   Have you ever tried to explain that to him?

*HENRY:*   Why should I?...Isn't the reason perfectly plain?

*JUDGE:*  To you, yes…But your REASON and his DESIRES can't possibly coincide …Therefore you've got to make HIS reasoning power work too…You've got to make him BELIEVE that staying out until midnight isn't good for him. And to do that you've got to make him reason it out for himself.

*PAUL:*  Great stuff, Judge…Dad, I'll bet ten dollars you don't know where Claud and Cliff are tonight?

*FANNY:*  Why of course we do, Paul…

*PAUL:*  Do you know, Dad?

*HENRY:*  I most certainly do…Your mother informed me before they went out this evening.

*PAUL:*  But neither of them told you, did they?

*HENRY:*  No Paul…I think it sufficient that they should tell their mother…

*HAZEL:*  Paul, I think you're horrid to talk to father like this…Just because you were shot down in the war you seem to think…

*FANNY:*  Hazel, please…Paul has asked you never to bring up the war in connection with himself…

*PAUL:*  *(grimly)* It's a nice little habit of Hazel's…

*FANNY:*  Let's not talk about it anymore…Paul, Claud and Cliff have gone down the Peninsula to the Roberts' summer home…They promised to be in by one… The Roberts are perfectly lovely people.

*PAUL:*  The Roberts' summer place, eh…*(chuckles)*

*(SOUND OF TELEPHONE)*

*HAZEL:*  I can reach it…I'll answer…*(pause)*…Hello?…Hello is that you, Cliff?… *(pause)*…What?…*(pause)*…Oh I'M sorry…I mistook you for my brother…Just a moment…Someone wants to talk to you, Paul.

*PAUL:*  Excuse me please…Thanks Hazel…Hello!…*(pause)*…Yes…Yes…I see…I see…*(pause)*…*(abruptly)* Well, keep the rest of it until I get there…Where are you?…Alright…Stand by…I'll be along…Goodbye.

(HANGS UP RECEIVER)

*HAZEL:*  If that wasn't Cliff's voice…

*PAUL:*  *(irritably)* You've got the most obnoxious imagination, Hazel…Mother, will you please excuse me…It's a most important call…

*FANNY:*  Of course, Paul…*(anxiously)*…I hope there's nothing the matter, dear…

*PAUL:* No, don't you worry...Dad, may I use your car for a couple of hours...I let the twins have mine for the night.

*HENRY:* *(grumbles)* It seems very strange that you should be having sudden calls at midnight, Paul.

*PAUL:* *(brusquely)* If you'd rather I didn't take it I'll call a taxi.

*HENRY:* *(grudgingly)* Oh, you're welcome to it...

*PAUL:* Thanks...You'll excuse me, won't you Judge...

*JUDGE:* Of course, Paul.

*PAUL:* It's been a real pleasure to see you again...Good night everyone...

(SOUND OF TAPPING OF CANE FADING OUT OF PICTURE)

("DESTINY WALTZ")

*MAC:* *(Irish)* They're in the receivin' room, Paul...Right in here!

(SOUND OF CANE TAPPING)

*PAUL:* Lead on Sarge.

(SOUND OF DOOR OPENING)

*PAUL:* *(cheerfully)* Hello kids...I mean to say, thinking of taking up permanent residence in the Burlingame city prison?

*CLAUD:* *(coming to mike)* Oh Paul...Paul.

*PAUL:* Oh I say, Claud...Take things easy...Things aren't so bad...How about it, Cliff?

*CLIFF:* *(gloomily)* They're pretty bad, Paul.

*PAUL:* Mind shutting the door, Sarge...

(SOUND OF DOOR CLOSING)

*PAUL:* Alright now, everyone grab himself a seat...I brought Police Sergeant McCurdy along to hear the sad tale.

*CLIFF:* Hello Sergeant.

*MAC:* *(dryly)* Good evenin', my boy...Seems loike old times whin I was doin' patrol duty in your neighborhood...Many's the time Oi got you out of scrapes when ye were a small tad.

*CLIFF:* Yeah...But nothing like this.

*PAUL:*   So you shot John Roberts, did you?

*CLAUD:*   He did NOT...It was I.

*PAUL:*   Better and better...I mean to say, nineteen's pretty young to start shooting up your men though, kid.

*CLIFF:*   *(belligerent)* Well, he had it coming...

*PAUL:*   Look here, let's have the whole story...By the way, I might add that the Burlingame police seem to be thoroughly mystified as to who did the shooting... So don't spill it after we get out of here.

*CLAUD:*   Then...then how did YOU know?

*PAUL:*   Just a shot in the dark...Heard at the desk that young Roberts had been shot and had an idea...that was all...Now then, from the beginning...

*CLIFF:*   What about Sergeant McCurdy?...Won't he have to report what we tell?

*MAC:*   This ain't my territory, Son...Besides, I wished Oi had a red cint for everything Oi've disremembered.

*PAUL:*   You begin Claud...

*CLAUD:*   Well...it...it started when John suggested that I go with him downstairs to his gun room...

*PAUL:*   Just a moment...How many were there at this party?

*CLIFF:*   About 30...

*PAUL:*   Including the old folks?...

*CLIFF:*   There wasn't any old folks.

*PAUL:*   What about servants?

*CLIFF:*   There weren't any servants...

*PAUL:*   *(dryly)* That's what I thought...Must have been a good party.

*CLIFF:*   It was until...until John got fresh with Claud.

*PAUL:*   That was down in the gun room, I suppose?

*CLAUD:*   Yes.

*PAUL:*   You two were alone?

*CLAUD:*   Yes...You see, I thought it would be alright...Everyone was jolly and we had the run of the house and...and so when John suggested we slip away and go down stairs I followed him.

*PAUL:*   Quite natural...You'd never suspect a host of being anything but a good sport as well as a good host...*(cynically)*...Too bad it doesn't usually work out that way.

*CLAUD:*   That's what I found out...Well, as soon as we got down there he grabbed me and kissed me...

*PAUL:*   I hope you didn't shoot him for that.

*CLAUD:*   No, of course not...I'm a good sport, I hope...I didn't even say anything when he mauled me a little...

*PAUL:*   Mauled, eh?...So that's what they do now days?

*MAC:*   They call it a lot of things these days, Paul...But Oi be thinkin' it's still the old-fashioned spoonin'.

*PAUL:*   *(chuckles)* I guess you're right at that, Mac...Well, let's have the rest of it, youngster.

*CLAUD:*   Then he said something to me.

(PAUSE)

*PAUL:*   *(casually)* Uh huh!

*CLAUD:*   I told him to leave me alone, and I started for the door.

*PAUL:*   Bad business...I mean to say, never take your eyes off a wild animal...Stare 'em out of countenance...A girl with nerve can stare herself out of a lot of bad situations.

*CLAUD:*   He ran after me and grabbed me and I jerked away from him and got a glass showcase between us...There was a lot of guns in it.

*PAUL:*   Enter the gun...I hope you wiped the fingerprints off it after you got through with it.

*CLAUD:*   I did.

*PAUL:*   *(astonished)* YOU *DID*!

*CLAUD:*   *(surprised)* Why yes, of course.

*MAC:*   Well, Oi'll be a sonofagun...Can ye beat that.

*PAUL:*   *(marvels)* Did I mention something about nerve?...Well, what happened?

*CLAUD:*   I reached into the case and pulled out a pistol and told John to keep away and let me alone or I'd shoot.

*PAUL:*   Quite the right procedure...Technique's above reproach so far...What about it, Mac?

*MAC:* *(grunts)*

*CLAUD:* Then...*(hesitates)*...Well, he laughed at me and said the gun wasn't loaded and leaned across the case and grabbed my hand and...and...I pulled the trigger.

*PAUL:* *(finishing thought)*...and young Mr. Roberts was mistaken...The gun WAS loaded.

*CLAUD:* *(dully)* Yes...

*PAUL:* At this point you calmly polished the gun off on your handkerchief and replaced it in the cabinet...

*CLAUD:* No...On my step-ins...

*PAUL:* On your...

(PAUL AND MAC BURST INTO ROAR OF LAUGHTER)

*PAUL:* But my dear child, why did you do that?

*CLAUD:* Because the gun was oily and I didn't want to get it on anything that would show.

*PAUL:* But wouldn't your underskirt have done just as well?

*CLAUD:* I didn't have any on.

*PAUL:* Well...*(bursts into fresh laughter)*...Mac, what do you think of my sister?

*MAC:* *(chuckles)* You can't beat this younger generation, Paul...Oi've said it before and Oi say it again...They'll go ye wan better eviry time.

*PAUL:* And after you replaced the gun, young woman...Then what happened?

*CLAUD:* The crowd was running down stairs...I didn't have a chance to get out of the room, so I hid in a closet.

*CLIFF:* I heard the shot upstairs...Everyone did...When we opened the door in the gun room and found John wounded and unconscious there was an awful scramble...

*CLAUD:* Yes, and when everyone was crowding around John, I sneaked out of the closet and joined them...

*CLIFF:* He was only shot in the shoulder.

*PAUL:* Yes, I know...Then no one knows who shot the boy but us and young Roberts, himself.

*CLIFF:* That's all and John won't dare tell...He's been in bad before and he knows that if it ever gets out just what happened and causes a scandal, his father will take his car and allowance away from him...Mr. Roberts has threatened to already...

*PAUL:*  Then you can depend upon Roberts to tell a suitable story when he comes to?

*CLIFF:*  You bet...

*MAC:*  But where are all the others...Did they all run out on ye?

*CLIFF:*  I should say not...We all stuck together...They brought us all down here and their folks came and got them...Most of them live down here on the Peninsula...

*PAUL:*  Released in care of their parents, eh?

*CLIFF:*  Yes...

*CLAUD:*  Paul, you didn't tell Mother and Dad where we were, did you?

*CLIFF:*  *(reproving)* Of course he didn't...

*PAUL:*  No, and if I were you youngsters I'd keep pretty quiet about it.

*CLAUD:*  Gee, I'm glad...They wouldn't understand...They...they'd think I did wrong to shoot him...

*PAUL:*  Well, what about it...Didn't you?

*CLAUD:*  *(defiantly)* Do you think I did?

*PAUL:*  *(evasive)* The law says you did...

*CLAUD:*  *(defiantly)* Well, I'm not sorry...He had it coming...

*CLIFF:*  *(anxiously)* Are you gonna get us out of here without making a row?

*PAUL:*  What about it Mac...think you can get the twins' names erased from the blotter and keep the thing covered up without too much juggling?

*MAC:*  Yeah, but they won't stay off long if young Roberts squawks...

*CLIFF:*  Listen Sergeant, I tell you I KNOW he won't open his mouth...

*MAC:*  Oi don't know about it...He sounds loike a contimptable rat to me.

*CLAUD:*  *(defiantly)* He is not...Just too fresh!

*MAC:*  Well can you beat that...Shootin' a guy and then defendin' him.

*PAUL:*  *(chuckles)* Just fresh, eh?

CLAUD: *(defiantly)* Yes. It's just between John and me...He lost and will be a good sport about it...You'll see!

PAUL: I tell you what, Mac...If he shows signs of weakening spill him an earful of what happens to little boys who give wild parties in this year of our Lord, 1932...I mean to say, your uniform will add a lot of weight to your words...

MAC: Well, we'll see, Paul...

PAUL: Come on, you kids...Get on your coats...You're going home in my car... Just as though nothing had happened. I've got Dad's machine.

CLIFF: Gee Paul, you're a good egg...Thanks awfully.

CLAUD: You do me more good than a million of Dad's lectures...

PAUL: Mind now you don't get into any more trouble on the way home...Come on, Mac...

(SOUND OF CANE FADING INTO DISTANCE)

("DESTINY WALTZ")

FANNY: Eat your eggs, Henry, while they're still hot...Here, have this wholewheat toast...

HENRY: But why isn't Jack down to breakfast?

FANNY: He'll be down, Henry...Did you and Clifford have a nice time at the Roberts' party last night, Claudia?

CLAUD: *(moodily)* Aaaw, it was alright.

PAUL: *(mocking)* I hope you acted like a lady, Claud.

CLAUD: *(blandly)* Sure, why not?

PAUL: Oh, I was just wondering...Can't tell what mischief kids will get into these days...

CLAUD: *(calmly)* Well, you'll notice they usually find SOME way of getting out.

FANNY: Why, what sort of trouble COULD a good girl get into at a nice home like the Roberts?

PAUL: That's alright, mother, I was just ragging Claud...

FANNY: Here's Jack now...Come to the table, Sonny...

HENRY: *(irritably)* Jack, don't you know you're to be down at eight o'clock sharp for breakfast?

JACK: Yes sir...I was out in the garden...I didn't know it was so late...Here, sir...I brought the paper in off the steps...

In the garden at Sea Cliff *(from left to right),* Claudia and Clifford, Mother Barbour
(in chair), Paul, Hazel, Father Barbour, Jack.

*HENRY:* *(grunts)* Well sit down and eat or you'll be late for school.

*JACK:* Yes sir...Mother, may I have my eggs boiled instead of poached this morning?

*FANNY:* Yes dear...Go out into the kitchen and ask Jenny to fix them.

*JACK:* Yes ma'am...*(leaving mike)* And may I have strawberry jam?

*HENRY:* This crab-apple jelly should do very nicely...

*JACK:* *(distance)* Yes sir.

*FANNY:* Henry, you're not going to say anything more about Jack's secret society I hope?

*HENRY:* What!...Of course...He'll think I'm a weak sort of father to let the matter drop...

*FANNY:* *(sighs)* Very well...You know what is best.

*PAUL:* *(amused)* Would you like me to hold him so you can hit him harder, sir?

*FANNY:* *(sharply)* Paul, that's enough...

*PAUL:* I'm sorry Dad...I beg your pardon.

*HENRY:* Never mind, Paul...Someday, when you're a father yourself, you'll understand better just what I'm up against.

*PAUL:* Sir, I don't think I'll ever have the nerve to try...It looks to me to be the most thankless task in the world...

*HENRY:* Please excuse me...If I don't glance at the headlines and stock market now, I'll not see it today...

(SOUND OF RATTLING PAPER)

*FANNY:* Go ahead and read your paper, Dear...

*HENRY:* *(surprise)* Why, what's this...*(reads)* "HOST SHOT AT PENINSULA PARTY"

*CLAUD:* *(gasps)* Father!

*HENRY:* *(reads)* "John Roberts Jr. Wounded During Fete of Younger Set!"...Clifford, Claudia get from that table and come into my den immediately.

*CLAUD:* *(frightened)* But Father...*(listlessly)* Oh very well!

*ANN:* You have just heard the first episode of "ONE MAN'S FAMILY" written for radio by Carlton E. Morse. The second episode entitled "The Younger Generation Messes Around" will be brought to you next Friday at 9:30 p.m. Pacific Time.

# CHAPTER THREE

## Mother Barbour's Recipe for Happiness

### DEDICATION

My dear Joan, this book is dedicated to you and the new family you are beginning; in a larger sense it is a dedication to our American way of life. You as a parent, you as a family unit, represent what America is going to be tomorrow. To feed a man is inspiring work, but to feed him spiritually and morally as well as physically is all of a woman's work.

*Dear Granddaughter Joan:*

When I married your grandfather, Henry Wilson Barbour, in San Francisco in 1896, I was just 18 years old and my mother and father said to me, "Fanny Martin, why in the world do you want to marry a sixteen-dollar-a-week bank clerk when you could have either that rising young attorney, Glenn Hunter, or young Doctor Fred Thompson?"[1]

Well, I didn't want Fred Thompson because he forever smelled of anesthetic—for an 18-year-old girl that was good reason for not being in love. And every girl in San Francisco knew that Glenn Hunter might be rising in the legal world but he also had a roving eye.

So I married your grandfather and now, looking back over 56 years of married life I can't help thinking how astute a girl sometimes can be in

---

[1] *The following family history is excerpted from a long letter written to Joan by Mother Barbour. The original appeared in* Mother Barbour's Favorite Recipes, *a premium issued on the occasion of "Family" celebrating its 20th anniversary on the air in 1952.*

arranging her own future. Before I had definitely announced my decision, however, Fred and Glenn and your grandfather, all good friends, were invariably Wednesday and Sunday evening visitors at the Martin home.

In the years since our marrige your grandfather went from bank clerk to a small building and loan business of his own on Sansome Street, and then to his own stock and bond business on Montgomery Street. Out of the bond business he built both a financial success and a prominent place in San Francisco for himself and his family. Strangely enough, neither Glenn, now Judge Glenn Hunter, nor Dr. Fred Thompson, ever married. Fred has been our family physician since the birth of Paul and has not only brought all my five children into the world but has officiated at the births of my 13 grandchildren. I hope he will attend you, Joan, when my first great-grandchild arrives.

At the turn of the century, Paul was about three years old and Hazel was on the way. Your grandfather had just got a precarious toehold in stocks and bonds on Montgomery Street, when Paul began to show signs of a touchy stomach. I'm sure now it was nothing important because he outgrew it in a year or so, but added to his upsets, and the fact that Hazel was making *me* a little squeamish sometimes, what should happen but your grandfather developed nervous indigestion because of business ups and downs? Well, out of our combined stomach "delicacy" I hit upon a dish that suited everyone. And I might add, in the past 50 years since then, we've never waited for a "weak stomach" to come along to revive the dish. It's good anytime for any kind of stomach. It's called Cream Chicken Soup Souffle, and let me recommend it.

Paul Barbour

We were living in a tiny house on Ellis Street near Leavenworth when Paul was born. Our fortunes began to improve as the Montgomery Street business began to grow, so your grandfather moved us out into the new Fillmore district. Now we had a kitchen, dining room, parlor and *two bedrooms*.

Well, from 1900 to 1912 I was a busy, happy housewife thinking that Paul and Hazel were the entire Barbour progeny. Your grandfather was engrossed in pursuing his stock and bond business to the top, and it was at about this time that we moved from the Fillmore district out beyond Golden Gate Park to a new development that still didn't have a name, but later became St. Francis Woods. We now had a Rambler automobile, and whether your grandfather got home at 6:00 in the evening or midnight depended on whether the cranky old thing would run. Then one day in mid-1911 I went to see Doctor Thompson and he said it looked suspiciously like we were to be parents again. That's when your grandfather started calling Fred "an old pill peddler," and he's never stopped to this day. However, Fred was right.

In 1912 there were no special tests to predict multiple births, so you can imagine my surprise when along came your mother, Claudia, and thirteen minutes later Clifford arrived. Your grandfather and I were as unprepared as two little babes lost in the woods. In the first place, we'd got out of the habit of infants in the household, what with your Uncle Paul by then 12 and your Aunt Hazel nine, but the twins turned out to be as much fun as they were work, and from that time forth both your grandfather and I decided that so long as we lived there should always be small children in our house. That's why grandchildren are so important to us and why your grandfather is so delighted over the prospect of the great-grandchild you are bringing us.

It was shortly after the twins were born that your grandfather decided he'd finally found the one and only spot in San Francisco to raise his ever increasing family—Sea Cliff! Well, there was an awful lot of discussion, because in those days Sea Cliff was still an undeveloped, barren landscape and transportation was practically nil. But it was beautiful. Sunday after Sunday we used to drive out and stand on the cliffs looking over the Golden Gate and out onto the Pacific. Finally we selected three lots and built a house. It's the same home we live in today. I remember so well the summer the house was being constructed, because our daily visits to the new place interfered considerably with my usual kitchen schedules. As a result, the family ate more salads for lunch and dinner than anytime before or since.

As you know, it was in the Sea Cliff house that your Uncle Jack was born in 1917, five years after Clifford and Claudia came along. We had decided that a family of four children was a nice round number and had settled down to enjoy them, when out of nowhere came this new baby knocking at our door. Your Aunt Hazel was just turning 17 and was highly indignant. I can still hear her say, "Mother, what are the girls going to think! The mother of a 17-year-old girl having a baby!"

On the other hand, Paul was all in favor of it. He was in his junior year at the University and even in those days had that wonderful quality of sensing other people's feelings.

Paul left the University to enlist the same year that Jack was born. You know the story, Joan, of how Paul was shot down in France and for many years thereafter walked with cane. His poor leg still shows deep, ugly scars.

But that wasn't the only hurt Paul got in the war; he found a young American Army nurse working in a hospital near his flying base in France and they fell in love. Her name was Elaine Hunter. They were secretly married in France, and it was only two weeks later that Paul was shot down. During that same week meningitis swept the hospital and poor Elaine, worked to exhaustion, came down with it and died. That was the *real* scar Paul brought home with him. He was so thin when he came home, poor boy, it was a pleasure to feed him up. You can do the same with Ross; he needs feeding up badly. If your meat budget is low, this Meat Loaf will do the trick. This is what your Aunt Hazel used to give Bill Herbert down on the dairy ranch when they were first married and were trying to make farming pay the bills. That was in the days before all the help from Washington to the farmers, and it was really hard going. Hazel and William married at the end of 1932.

Your mother and father married earlier, in 1931. It's hard for me to think of them as *your* parents, Joan darling; they were such children themselves. I *am* sorry your father never lived for you to know him because he was the most maddeningly handsome, most devil-may-care, most aristocratic-looking young man I ever knew. You get your own good looks from him as much as from Claudia. I'm sure if he were living today, he would be as happy about you as we all are—the way you've settled down to be a good wife, looking forward to motherhood so calmly and graciously.

And now for the Sour Cream Pie. This is the pie with which Jack wooed Betty Carter all through high school. I had to make a pie once a week and Jack lugged it over to Betty's house. Not that Betty was such a pie eater, but her father was. He made a deal with Jack that he would not interfere with Jack's interest in Betty so long as he got one of my pies each week. This went on until Jack and Betty went down to Stanford to college.

You know there was an awful hassle over the twins' names when Hazel had them in the hospital. Jack came in, took one look at them, and named the red-headed one Pinky and other one Hank! Hazel cried and Bill went back to the dairy ranch mad at everybody. Of course, their right names are Henry Barbour Herbert and William Martin Herbert, but in spite of everything, Hank and Pinky stuck. Now Hazel uses the nicknames the same as everyone else.

Well, my dear, by the time you came along in 1933 your father, Johnny, had died and Claudia was home but at loose ends. Strangely, as it seems now, you were not born at the Barbour house. Claudia was down the Peninsula visiting the day the stork arrived. I remember so well; it was a bitter, stormy night and Dr. Thompson had one awful time getting down to Claudia. That same night you came into the world, your Grandmother Roberts had another of her heart attacks and died less than five minutes after you were placed in her arms.

And that's where your great wealth came from. I never did know exactly how much she left you but it was rumored to be in the neighborhood of $400,000. I think you are so wise to just let it lie and live off Ross's salary as

Hazel bathing the twins, Pinky and Hank.

he wants you to. You both will be happier not having your lives involved with a clutter of money at this stage.

While your mother and your Aunt Hazel were having grandchildren for your grandfather and me, your Uncle Paul had become interested in a lovely widow named Beth Holly. We thought for years they were going to marry. Beth was as much a part of the family as an actual daughter-in-law. But in the end they didn't marry, and bit by bit they drifted apart. I mention Beth because she is the only girl Paul came near marrying in all the years since Elaine's death.

My goodness, I forgot all about Paul's adoption of Teddy. It just occurred to me that Paul found Teddy the same year you were born, and in one way it was Teddy who was responsible for the separation of Paul and Beth. She was an enchanting little girl and Beth refused to go into competition with a seven-year-old.

Teddy

In 1937, Clifford married Ann Waite. The day that your grandfather rented Claudia's and Johnny's honeymoon house to Professor Waite and his daughter Ann, was the most tragic day in the history of the Barbour family. The professor was head of the Music Department at the University; Ann was a child piano prodigy and had grown up into a young woman who knew nothing—*nothing at all*—but her piano and her music. And Clifford had to fall in love with her! I *will* say *this* for Professor Waite: he had one good recipe which I'll give you, but beyond that he was a narrow, arrogant, dictatorial man who had made an automaton out of Ann and had nipped all her normal feminine instincts before they even budded.

Clifford

When your Uncle Clifford married Ann and she was suddenly brought out of her childish dream world and face to face with physical and human love, she was confused and terrified. She called Clifford a clod and a beast. Naturally their marriage lasted exactly long enough for Ann to pack her clothes and rush back across the bay to Berkeley, where her father had taken a house after the marriage. That was the last time Clifford ever saw Ann alive. Unbeknownst to him, she was going to have a baby, but the baby was born and Ann died before he was aware of either event. Ann did not die in childbirth as so many people think. It was a normal and easy time for her, according to her doctor, but she made a desperate attempt to get out of the hospital and run back to her father's house the same day the baby was born, and that is what brought about her death.

Well after Ann died Professor Waite did not want the baby, so your grandfather and I went to the hospital and got him. He was a beautiful boy, but Clifford was so wrought up over Ann he could not bear the sight of the child. It was almost a year before we finally got him to take an interest. Even then, he didn't give him a name, just called him Skip or Skipper until the boy was almost eight years old.

Then the boy and his father got together and decided on Andrew after his mother Ann. Now he's called Andy. He's such an industrious little fellow. He's 14 now and going to boarding school down near Mountain View and working in Mr. Smithers' drugstore.

Whenever Andy comes up for a weekend to stay with his grandfather and me, I usually try to invite Margaret, your little sister, Penny, and Jack's three eldest daughters Elizabeth Sharon Ann, Janie and Mary Lou over for Sunday morning breakfast.

Goodness, I really got ahead of myself talking about your sister Penelope and Jack's three elder daughters. Let's see, your mother married Captain Nicholas Lacey in 1935—and how we all loved dear Nicky. Penny was born in 1938, the year after Andy. Then Jack's children were born, if I remember, as follows: Elizabeth Sharon Ann in 1942, Janie in 1943, and Mary Lou in 1944. You remember that your mother gave the honeymoon house across the hedge from the family home to Jack and Betty as a wedding present. That was after Ann died and Clifford came back home to live.

My, what a struggle Jack and Betty have had maintaining it. After college, Jack went into Judge Hunter's law office and the children began to come. Both Jack and Betty were "poor but proud" and would accept no help whatsoever from your grandfather.

When Jack and Betty's triplets, Abbie, Debby and Connie arrived, Betty really went into her "stretcher recipes." The triplets came as a New Year's present, Abigail being born ten minutes before midnight, 1948, Deborah right on the stroke of midnight, and Constance 12 minutes into the New Year of 1949. What a time Jack and Betty had with their "six beautiful daughters," as Jack always insists on calling them.

But there I go getting ahead of myself again. The triplets came after Jack's three years in the Armed Services, and what a time Betty had with the three older girls while Jack was away. That's when she really became a good cook, "preparing herself for Jack's return," as she put it, and also giving herself something to keep her mind off Jack's absence.

Here I am telling you about what happened in 1949 and I haven't said a word about Bill Herbert dying and leaving your Aunt Hazel a widow back in 1940 when you, Hank and Pinky were still such little folk. I forgot to mention that Hazel's daughter Margaret was born in 1936, three years after Hank and Pinky.

Hazel did a wonderful job with Hank, Pinky and Margaret without a father. Then in 1945 she married Daniel Murray. What a blessing he was; not only for Hazel but for the three children.

Now that I start thinking back over the family history, I think of Irene, Clifford's second wife. What a lovely, lovely girl she was. I think Clifford's

Captain Nicholas Lacey and Claudia on their wedding day, 1935.

whole life would have been different if she hadn't been killed so tragically in that wicked automobile accident. Do you remember that Clifford married Irene Franklin in 1942, and after only four years, lost her in 1946?

Well, the years have gone by. Poor Teddy, or perhaps I should say happy, happy Teddy. She's doing noble work these days. When she grew old enough to know her mind, she found that few men had the high ideals of her adopted father, Paul. So she turned to nursing and became an Army nurse. She's now stationed over in Japan under Major Edith Aynes, devoting all her love to taking care of our boys hurt in Korea. She *did* try marriage once, with Elwood Giddings, but it just didn't work.

And do you know, I got a letter from Pinky the other day? He certainly is having a time as a sailor boy stationed at the Brooklyn Navy Yard. He was remembering the old summer vacations at the Sky Ranch and asked if I still made that "lovely" Sky Ranch Salad.

And Hank, bless his heart, over at the University of California, is working his way through medical school and doing so well in his studies. I don't know why he won't let his grandfather help him a little with money, but he won't and we're certainly just as proud of him as your Aunt Hazel is.

I was interrupted just now by Betty on the phone. She says she's afraid the triplets are coming down with measles. What a life! She also said if I left my Salmon Mousse recipe out of this list to you, she'd never forgive me. How she can think of Salmon Mousse with the threat of measles-in-triplicate in the offing I don't know, but that's Betty.

And now, my dear, I think I'd better end this list of recipes right here. I hope that some of them will become favorites in your family as they have in mine, and I know that, as the years pass, you will find many to add to this list. I like to think that sometime in the future you will be compiling such a list for *your* grandchildren, along with your "special memories" of your fine family. May those memories bring you as much comfort and pleasure as mine do.

*Your grandmother,*

**Fanny Barbour**

Cover of an early promotional booklet created by a sponsor.

# CHAPTER FOUR

## America's Heartland: The "Family" Audience

The success of "One Man's Family" derived in large part from its realism. The Barbours were real, or at least that is how most people wanted to see them. The themes that Carlton E. Morse wrote into his scripts for the first 18 years were those most families dealt with on a day-to-day basis. These ideas were conveyed with humor supported by a helpful philosophy. Michael Raffetto, a cast member and in the last nine years a writer with Morse and Harlan Ware, believed that in addition to the series' inherent qualities, its initial appearance during the Depression was a factor in its popularity:

> "Starting in 1932, in the very depth of the Depression, it gave people hope and a goal. Here was an ideal family, united, loving and seemingly real, that wasn't ground down with financial worries. I can't remember that the Depression was ever mentioned in the scripts. The problems were the universal ones of adolescence, love, and bewilderment in the rearing of children, but never of wondering where the next meal was coming from. It was the kind of family everyone wanted to identify with. There was always money enough, and when a transgressor couldn't get understanding from Father Barbour, there was always Paul...who understood and forgave...the perfect father figure that old and young alike never really stop searching for..."

Most of the show's listeners, if asked what effect they thought the "Family" had on them, would probably reply in a similar vein to these comments from a fan letter:

> "...[W]e are regular listeners to the "One Man's Family" program and have been for many years. We live their lives with them, absorbing the fine philosophy adaptable in anybody's family! In that half-hour broadcast, we often see ourselves as others see us, and in so doing we get a broader and entirely different slant on similar situations."

Conversely to the show's impact on its audience, did audience reaction affect Morse and his script writing? Listeners did write frequently to comment on story development, but Morse has said that most of the cases where the audience did influence him concerned "trivial things" that he does not now remember.

However, there was a time when Morse listened *very* carefully. To his cast! This was the reason for the 27-year run of the show, and the main reason for the loyalty of the original players. It had long been Morse's need to cast and direct all of his shows. With "One Man's Family" there was a wonderful relationship between the players and Morse. As he tells it in his own words:

> "I would begin with a tiny suggestion of a plot idea which I would write into a half-hour script. I then would sit down at a rehearsal and listen to the various voices as they read their lines. Suddenly a tone of voice, a happy association of my words and the actors giving deeper meaning to the script, told me instinctively what the next episode must contain. This way, week after week, I would give the cast something to build on. And each time they would add something more. So we moved deeper and deeper, higher and higher, until we created a peak of interest. Our cooperative intimacy extended and entered homes not only in the United States and Canada, but even in Russia where it was played for years on radio both to teach Russians English, and to tell them how the American family lived."

Morse's sensitivity to audience opinion was evidently well-founded. In the early days of the program, some listeners wrote to complain that the scripts were becoming too sexually explicit. NBC was not prepared to field such criticism and urged Morse in strong terms to censor himself. This correspondence is probably one of the earliest instances of broadcast censorship; it clearly shows, as well, the mindset of a notable segment of "Family" listeners.

"One Man's Family" garnered many awards and honors in its 27 years on the air. NBC once described it as "radio's most honored drama show." On April 27, 1952, the network celebrated the series' 20th anniversary with a special half-hour radio program, "Twenty Years with the Barbours"; it featured, among other stars, Phil Harris, Alice Fay and Bob Hope. In keeping with the occasion, the Barbours' "home town" of San Francisco declared April 29 "One Man's Family" Day.

MISC 12-8-33

TO Mr Carlton Morse

FROM   Don E Gilman

SUBJECT

DATE Apr 27 1935

 

 

 

The attached copy of a letter has been sent to me from New York  I think there is serious danger in these scenes which become too intimate.

There is at the present moment forming a league of decency similar to that which was organized around the Motion Picture Industry, and I know you would not want "One Man's Family" to be regarded by this League as an undesirable program.

In other words, in my opinion, there is a definite threat in this letter which we should take seriously.

Don E Gilman

<u>COPY</u>

Hotel Lafayette
Buffalo  N Y
April 4  1935

President
National Broadcasting Co
New York

Dear Sir:

I voice the protest that clean-minded men and women, everywhere, feel against the sex filth that you are permitting "One Man's Family" to broadcast.

The radio audience of America had come to enjoy and love this feature in the original state, when its characters faithfully portrayed bits of daily life common in all of our homes.

But about six weeks ago, the tenor of this feature changed - it no longer was the clean, bright, entertaining material to which whole families could look forward and enjoy. We began to hear "in bed" confidences of husband and wife - so frightfully intimate, that one gasped, in anticipation of what might be next - and expelled the children of the family from the living rooms. And then Hazel began to demonstrate nude baths on the front porch and Father Barbour began to examine his son's fiancee's hosiery. All this stuff we listened to, hoping that it would soon be over, but when in this week's broadcast, Claudia and her brother exchanged confidences, and the former said she married hastily because she <u>could</u> <u>not</u> <u>wait</u> <u>to</u> <u>learn</u> <u>of</u> <u>life's</u> <u>experiences,</u> etc. etc. ad infinitum, the climax was reached, and women everywhere tuned out instantly. This may be a small matter, but I can assure you that the women of America are sharply placing the stamp of disapproval on National Broadcasting features.

This feature has changed sponsors many times recently -- have you ever considered that one solution may be that women and children do not listen to material of that kind - and that sponsors depending on advertising through that source, are <u>the</u> <u>suffer-</u> ers. We liked the nice, clean-minded Barbour family - but club women everywhere frown upon the filth and lust which the NBC is now broadcasting into millions of homes through this feature.

Evidently, it's the author who needs to be jacked up before a public protest is made against NBC.

Yours very truly,

(signed)  Ma??? L. Fa??????

NATIONAL BROADCASTING COMPANY, Inc.
# INTERDEPARTMENT CORRESPONDENCE

TO     Mr Carlton Morse                          DATE   October 14 1935

FROM   Don E Gilman

SUBJECT

I feel that you are treading on very dangerous ground with the trend of the continuity in "One Man's Family". I am confronted with an increasing number of queries such as one which was put to me last night before last night's program by a man who is a regular and loyal listener. He said "how far is this sex trend in "One Man's Family" going to go? It has been so free from this sort of thing in the past that I regret to see it creeping into the continuity."

It is true that what is said detached from the scene is not objectionable, but the suggestion of naked bodies and men and women going to bed together and scenes in night clothes do suggest sex.

The danger you are running into is that a number of these complaints is going to interfer with the renewal of this contract next year.

Several of the bedroom scenes lately could just as well been living room, dining room or any other room scenes and did not need to suggest the intimate relationship between men and women.

I hope you will discontinue this type of presentation before we are asked to do so by our New York office if not the Federal Communications Commission. You may be sure it is going to bring forth many annoying complaints.

Don E Gilman

"One Man's Family" was unique among radio dramas of its day in that it deliberately set out to transmit a moral and social message to its audience. While Walter Sheppard and others have expressed the wish that "Morse had carried out his didactic purpose more subtly," the show's success suggests that listeners didn't mind being preached to, as long as they were also entertained. Indeed, for many people in the troubled '30s and '40s, a story with strong convictions about how life *ought* to be must have been profoundly reassuring.

# CHAPTER FIVE

# The Barbour Clan and Their Private New Year

**ANNOUNCEMENTS AND DESCRIPTIONS
FOR
"ONE MAN'S FAMILY"
CHAPTER TWELVE — BOOK FIFTY–TWO**

**"THE BARBOUR CLAN AND THEIR OWN PRIVATE NEW YEAR"**

**Sunday**                    **5:30-6:00 p.m.**        **December 31, 1944**

*(ORGAN)*

*ANNOUNCER:*   One Man's Family, brought to you by Fleischmann's Yeast!

(ORGAN)

*ANN:*   One Man's Family is dedicated to the Mothers and Fathers of the younger generation and to their bewildering offspring. Tonight we present Chapter Twelve, Book Fifty-two entitled, "THE BARBOUR CLAN AND THEIR OWN PRIVATE NEW YEAR"!

(ORGAN)

*ANN:*   What a year! WHAT A YEAR! Well anyway it's almost over now and in a few more hours will be entirely the property of historians. For if ever there was an

The Barbour family celebrates the New Year, December 31, 1944.

HISTORICAL year it was 1944 and '45 bids fair to be even more eventful...But that isn't why we're here tonight...To discuss historical events! No, this is New Year's Eve and all the Barbours and a couple of their friends have congregated up at the Sky Ranch to see the New Year in...Yes, Clifford and Irene (assisted by Skippy and old Ben) are the hosts for tonight's New Year's Eve Party...And everybody's present or accounted for, you may depend on it! Irene has pushed the big dining room table back against the wall in the living room and has loaded it down with good things to eat, buffet style! Eat as often and as much as nature and your own discretion will allow you! At this end of the table is a cold tom turkey with dressing and cranberry sauce; there's a plate of cold baked ham, pickles, cheese and olives to go with it...There's a heaping big bowl of red apples, a bowl of cracked nuts, a dish pan full of newly popped and buttered popcorn, a big pitcher of apple cider and another of creamy milk and fruitcake and pumpkin and mince pie and oh so many other goodies, you know that Clifford and Irene and Skippy and Ben must have had their sleeves rolled up in the kitchen most of the day in preparation.

(LOTS OF NEW YEAR'S EVE NOISE MAKERS)

*AD LIB:* *(noise)* Happy New Year...etc...

*CLIFF:* *(on cue)* Hey...Hey...Quiet...Quiet...

(RASPBERRY ON NOISEMAKER)

(LAUGHTER)

*CLIFF:* Okay Pinky stop snoring...

*BEN:* *(laughs)* Snoring he says...

(EVERYONE LAUGHS)

*CLIFF:* Okay, we've got about an hour to wait until midnight and the new year, and as master of ceremonies...

*HAZEL:* *(up)* Margaret come away from that table...Excuse me Cliff...

*CLIFF:* *(amused)* Sure, discipline before oratory...

(LAUGHTER)

*HAZEL:* *(up)* Did you hear me Margaret?

*MARGARET:* *(off)* I'm just having a piece of FRUITCAKE, Mommy...

*HAZEL:* *(up)* That's all you've been doing all evening...Having a piece of SOMETHING...

*PAUL:* *(amused)* Haven't we ALL...

*BETTY:* UH-HUH...

*HAZEL:* Margaret you'll have mollygrubbles all night...

*MARGARET:* *(coming to mike)* But I don't feel a BIT FULL Mommy, running around all the time and just NIBBLING...

*FANNY:* *(amused)* No, I don't think it'll hurt her Hazel...

*MARGARET:* THANK YOU, GRANDMOTHER

(LAUGHTER)

*HAZEL:* *(amused)* Nevertheless, you sit down here by me and let your stomach rest for a little...

*CLIFF:* Well, as I was about to say when so rudely interrupted...

*HAZEL:* I apologized for interrupting, Clifford...

*CLIFF:* *(amused)* Sure you did...I was only kidding...Well to begin all over again...

(RASPBERRY ON NOISEMAKER)

(LAUGHTER)

*CLIFF:* Somebody choke that Canadian goose!

(LAUGHTER)

*CLIFF:* Okay...This is the Barbour version of how to celebrate the New Year...As Irene and I warned everyone, we're going to put on our own New Year's Follies, with songs, dances and funny sayings...

(LAUGHTER)

*CLIFF:* And we'll begin right now, if Mom'll go to the piano...

*FANNY:* But YOU didn't tell me I was supposed to play, Clifford...

*CLIFF:* Sure...You're the official accompanist...

*PINKY:* Sure, go on Grandma...YOU can do it...

*FANNY:* *(amused)* Well maybe I can and maybe I can't...What am I supposed to do...

*CLIFF:* *(to everybody)* We're going to start tonight's entertainment by singing one verse of 'AMERICA'...

*SKIPPY:* *(eager)* I know that...I know that Mommy...

*IRENE:* Of course you do.

*MARGARET:*  *(scorn)* Sure, EVERYBODY does...

*CLIFF:*  So will everybody get to his feet...

(SCUFFLING AND MURMURED CONFUSION)

(PIANO STRIKES CHORD ON CUE)

(SLIGHT PAUSE THEN EVERYONE SINGS ONE VERSE OF 'AMERICA')

(MURMUR OF SELF APPRECIATION)

*TEDDY:*  Tony you're in wonderful voice tonight...

*TONY:*  *(amused)* Yes, I always sing well in a MOB...

*BEN:*  Anybody hear MY fog horn...I say, did anyone hear my fog horn blast out...

*BETTY:*  *(amused)* Oh sure, you sounded GOOD Ben...

*BEN:*  Thank you Miss Betty...Thank you...

*CLIFF:*  Okay, quiet everyone...Now the first member of our company I am calling on to entertain us this evening is a very good friend, although not exactly a member of the family...Except in spirit...Tony Bronson...

(SOUND OF CHEERS AND HAND CLAPPING)

*TONY:*  *(amused)* Well, you're certainly in a hurry about calling on the lesser lights, Clifford

*HANK AND PINKY:*  On your feet...Out in front...

*CLIFF:*  Yeah, come out here in front of people, Tony...

*TONY:*  *(coming to mike)* What are you trying to do, make an orator out of me...

*CLIFF:*  *(coming to mike)* There, that's better...Friends and family, I give you Tony...

*TEDDY:*  *(softly)* Atta boy, Tony...

*TONY:*  Well, when Clifford told me I was going to be called upon tonight I thought what I could say...As you people must know there's a great deal in my heart...Much to be thankful for! I came out of a Marine hospital six or eight months ago, weak and sick and...yes, AFRAID...I hardly knew which way to turn, and by some lucky chance I fell in your hands...Since that time my life has become more and more filled with the things every man wants for himself...I think 1944 was my lucky year...Yes, it was the year of my experience at Tarawa...the year of some agony and physical and mental disabilities; But out of that grew my relationship with the Barbours! I thank you for 1944 and I wish for you a VICTORIOUS AND A PROSPEROUS 1945, with the return of your loved ones, now away...I thank you...

*TEDDY:* *(on cue)* Tony that was BEAUTIFUL...

*TONY:* *(low)* I hope I didn't gush too much...

*TEDDY:* Oh no...You made my heart come right up in my throat...

*CLIFF:* *(off little)* Okay, our next entertainer this evening is my favorite son and heir, Mr. J.D. (Skipper) Barbour...IN PERSON!

(LAUGHTER AND HAND CLAPPING)

*IRENE:* Alright Skippy

*SKIPPY:* Did you mean ME, Daddy...Is it my turn?

*CLIFF:* *(coming to mike)* It most certainly IS...Come on out and I'll stand beside you.

*SKIPPY:* No, I want to go alone...

*CLIFF:* *(amused)* Well OKAY...Right out in the middle...

*SKIP:* Okay...

(PAUSE)

*CLIFF:* *(off little)* Okay, go ahead.

*SKIPPY:* I don't remember...

(LIGHT LAUGHTER)

*IRENE:* *(amused)* Oh sure you do Skippy...Beautiful hands...

*SKIPPY:* Oh yeah...
Beautiful hands are those that do
Work that is earnest and brave and true
Moment by moment the whole day through
Beautiful lips are those that say
The kindest things in the kindest way...

*CLIFF:* Good boy, Skip...

(LAUGHTER AND HAND CLAPPING)

*SKIPPY:* That isn't all...That's not all...

*IRENE:* *(off little)* Sure Skippy, that's all...

*SKIP:* No it isn't...As I was going to the garden gate...

*IRENE:* *(amused)* Oh oh...

*SKIP:*   I met a little garden snake
        He ate so much of my jelly cake
        It make his little belly ache…

(LAUGHTER)

*IRENE:*   Why Skippy, I never taught you that…

*SKIPPY:*   I know it…Ben did though.

*BEN:*   *(laughs)* Yep…Yep, I did at that…

*IRENE:*   Well Ben, I think you and I are going to have to get together on Skippy's education…

*BEN:*   I done wrong?…Don't say I done wrong on account it would just about bust my heart…

*CLIFF:*   *(amused)* Hey Irene, you couldn't bust Ben's heart on New Year's Eve…

(LAUGHTER)

*IRENE:*   *(amused)* No Ben, but we DO seem to have different tastes in poetry…

*BEN:*   *(agrees)* I'll bet we have at that, Mrs. Barbour…

(LIGHT LAUGHTER)

*CLIFF:*   And now New Year's Eve revelers…

(LAUGHTER)

*CLIFF:*   The next number on tonight's entertainment is Miss Margaret "Lily Pons" Herbert in an aria entitled, "THE MYSTERY"…

(LAUGHTER AND HAND CLAPPING)

*CLIFF:*   Right up here Margaret…

*MARGARET:*   Okay, *I* know where to come…

*TEDDY:*   The nonchalance of the very young…

*HENRY:*   Yes, yes…

*MARGARET:*   *(off little)* Everybody's got to keep still…

*CLIFF:*   *(leaving little)* Yes, quiet everybody…Let's have a little quiet…

(PAUSE)

(MARGARET SINGS "THE MYSTERY")

(SOUND OF APPLAUSE)

*BETTY, TEDDY, IRENE:* *(ad lib)* More...More

*CLIFF:* Yes, folks...Yes, she will sing again, later in the program...Thank you Miss Margaret "Schumann-Heink" Herbert for your excellent rendition...

(LAUGHTER)

*MARGARET:* *(softly)* Hey Mommy, is he making fun of me?

*HAZEL:* *(laughs)* Of course not, Darling...It's all just a lot of fun...

*MARGARET:* Oh...

*CLIFF:* *(off little)* All right friends, now that you have heard the daughter perform, I take extreme pleasure in presenting the MOTHER...

*HAZEL:* ME, already?

*CLIFF:* *(off little)* If you'll please come out in the circle...

*HAZEL:* *(coming to mike)* With a great deal of pleasure...

*CLIFF:* *(coming to mike)* The pleasure is mutual...Ladies and gentlemen, Mrs. Hazel Barbour Herbert will do a song and dance routine including the "Strawberry Blonde"...My sister Hazel...

(LAUGHTER AND HAND CLAPPING)

*HAZEL:* *(laughs)* I think Clifford has his announcements a little mixed...I'm neither singing NOR dancing...*(sobers)* In fact I'm going to do something I think is very fitting on this occasion and in this house. I'm going to read a poem which Nicholas Lacey wrote to Claudia while they were living right here...

(MURMUR OF APPROVAL AND INTEREST)

*HAZEL:* Many of you will remember it...I do VIVIDLY because the first time I ever heard it, Claudia took me up the redwood trail in back of the house here and we sat on a mossy old log. She was very much affected by it...This is what she read to me:
I have come to drink at the fountain of your beauty,
I have come to share with you the depths of our emotions.
Whiteness and softness are yours.
Surely no where will I find more of generousness and deep
Satisfaction.
Between you and me there is a bond.
There is a bond tempered by the seared heat of desire and
Hardened by the cold facts of mutual need.
In youthful eagerness I came to you and you knew me,
In maturity I still turn to you and you show no less of
Generosity.
Calmness and steadfastness are yours.
For with the advancing years when others come and go you
Change not.

Between you and me there is no wall;
There is no wall of discontent, nor is there a wall of
Hostility.
In all the days of our living there has been no wall.
And to the day of our dying there will be no wall.
Forever and ever, I love you.

(PAUSE)

*HAZEL:* That was Nicky's love poem to Claudia...The only one he ever wrote that
I know of...Thank you...

(PAUSE)

*JOAN:* *(on cue) (affected)* Hazel?

*HAZEL:* Yes Joan?

*JOAN:* I didn't know about that before...Could I have a copy of it?

*HAZEL:* Why of course you can...You may have this one in fact...

*JOAN:* I think that's very beautiful of them being in love that way...

*PAUL:* I think we all feel the same way Joan...

(SLIGHT MURMUR OF APPROVAL)

*JOAN:* Could I be next?

*CLIFF:* Well I'll bet you CAN, Joan...Step right up...

*JOAN:* *(coming to mike)* Okay...I just thought of a poem I wanted to say...

*CLIFF:* *(coming to mike)* Well come right ahead...

*JOAN:* This is the very first poem I can remember Claudia teaching me...It goes
like this:
With these bows upon my shoulder,
and these slippers on my feet,
I'm my Mommy's little darling, don't you think I'm sweet...
My little petticoat of lace, my pretty sash of blue,
My mommy made them for me, to say this piece to you...

(LAUGHTER AND CLAPPING)

*HENRY:* Yes, yes...I remember when she used to say that...

*PINKY:* Yeah, so do I...BOY did I think she was prissy...

*JOAN:* *(amused)* I guess I WAS kinda prissy in those days...*(sighs)* But Claudia
dressed me awfully PRETTY...

*HAZEL:* *(amused)* I should say she DID...

*CLIFF:* *(off little)* Alright...The next person to appear on this great one-night stand is Mr. Benjamin Findlay...

*BEN:* *(off little)* You mean ME?

*CLIFF:* *(amused)* Certainly I mean you...Right up here Ben...

*BEN:* *(coming to mike)* Well I only got two poems in my whole bag of tricks and Skippy went and said ONE of them...

*CLIFF:* *(amused)* Okay, then you can say the other one...

*BEN:* It's kind of shorty...

*CLIFF:* *(laughs)* Maybe you should say it twice to make it longer...

*BEN:* No...No...Once is enough...Ready?

*CLIFF:* *(amused)* Any time now...

*BEN:* Well here she is:
Fishy, fishy in the brook
Papa catch him with a hook,
Mama fry him in the pan.
Baby eat him like a man...

(LAUGHTER)

*BEN:* *(surprised)* Heey, they LIKED it...

*CLIFF:* *(amused)* Sure they did...

*BEN:* I'm a success...I AM A SUCCESS...

(LAUGHTER)

*CLIFF:* *(amused)* And now that we've had that great epic from the lips of Ben, I will next call on Pinky...

(ALL THE KIDS...YEAH, COME ON PINK...ATTA OLD KID PINK...ETC.)

*CLIFF:* Ladies and gentlemen, I introduce to you Pinky, known to his teachers as William Martin Herbert...Willy GIVE!

*PINKY:* Heey, nobody ever calls me Willy and lives to tell about it.

*CLIFF:* That's for giving me the raspberry on your tin-whistle awhile ago.

*PINKY:* Okay...We're even...

CLIFF: *(agrees)* Even-Stephen...And now what are YOU going to do for us this evening?

PINKY: A POME

CLIFF: *(amused)* Check...Pinky's going to do a POME!

(LIGHT LAUGHTER)

PINKY: I MUST NOT THROW UPON THE FLOOR
THE CRUST I CANNOT EAT
FOR MANY LITTLE HUNGRY ONES
WOULD FIND IT QUITE A TREAT
WILFUL WASTE MAKES WOEFUL WANT,
AND I MAY LIVE TO SAY
THAT I MAY WISH I HAD THE CRUST
THAT ONCE I THREW AWAY...

PAUL: Well, well...A plug for the O.P.A.

(LAUGHTER)

CLIFF: And now I think it's time we called on Paul...

(AD LIB AGREEMENT....CLAPPING)

CLIFF: Okay, I give you our brother, Paul...The boy with the high I.Q. and the LOW hair-line...

(LAUGHTER)

PAUL: *(amused)* I think we could undoubtedly have got ourselves a better master of ceremonies without extending ourselves...

CLIFF: Oh picking on the M.C., huh...

PAUL: A man with a big mouth and no volume control...

(LAUGHTER)

CLIFF: Friend, I'm in a position to do you a lot of harm...

(LAUGHTER)

PAUL: I'll remember that...Well to get down to the matter of the moment...When Clifford told me I would be expected to contribute tonight, I looked through my shelf of poetry for something appropriate...I found this poem by Robert Frost called, "The Road Not Taken"...It seemed a thoughtful consideration of our own situation with the beginning of the new year...With 1945 each of us are going to have the opportunity of walking one of two ways...It's going to be hard to choose which path to take...Well anyway, listen to what Robert Frost says:

Two roads diverged in a yellow wood,
And sorry I could not travel both
And be one traveler long I stood
And looked down one as far as I could
To where it bent in the undergrowth;

Then took the other one, as just as far,
And having perhaps the better claim,
Because it was grassy and wanted wear;
Though as for that the passing there
Had worn them really about the same,

And both that morning equally lay
In leaves no step had trodden black.
Oh, I kept the first for another day!
Yet knowing how way leads on to way,
I doubted if I should ever come back.

I shall be telling this with a sigh
Somewhere ages and ages hence:
Two roads diverged in a wood, and I—
I took the one less traveled by,
And that has made all the difference.

*IRENE:*   Oh *goood*!

*TEDDY:*   Paul, I never heard you read that before...

*TONY:*   *(agrees)* It's certainly a good thought for New Year's Eve...

*CLIFF:*   Okay, now let's hear from Betty...

*BETTY:*   *(off little)* Oh golly...ME?

*CLIFF:*   You bet...On your feet lady...

*BETTY:*   *(amused) (coming to mike)* But I'm only the mother of daughters, not an entertainer...

*CLIFF:*   Well, MOTHER OF DAUGHTERS, *face* your audience...

*BETTY:*   *(laughs)* Ooooh, LOTS of people, huh!

(LAUGHTER)

*BETTY:*   *(serious)* Look, honestly, I can't make a speech...I just want to make a New Year *wish*...I wish for Jack's return in 1945...I wish for the resumption of our home life, our marital relations, our place together in the world...I wish for the man I love to come home from the wars to help me bring up our three little girls in the GOOD way...in the Barbour tradition...And that's all...

(AD LIBS OF VERY GOOD...WONDERFUL BETTY...WE HOPE SO TOO...ETC)

*HENRY:*   Yes, yes...you gave a good account of yourself Betty...

*BETTY:*   Thank you Father Barbour...

*CLIFF:*   *(off little)* And now may I present our Cadet Nurse...Teddy, come up here...

(AD LIB ENCOURAGEMENT AND HAND CLAPPING)

*CLIFF:*   INTROOODUCIIING Cadet Nurse Teddy Barbour, the little girl with the big heart...

(LAUGHTER AND APPLAUSE)

*TEDDY:*   *(laughs)* I'm not so little at that! I unloaded a 170 pound patient from the operating room wagon and put him to bed all by myself...

*CLIFF:*   The lady says she has MUSCLES...

(LAUGHTER)

*TEDDY:*   Well, look, I'm not going to try to entertain you either...Like Betty, I just want to make a New Year's Wish...I hope that the next time we celebrate New Year's Eve this same group will all be together...

*BETTY:*   *(off little)* Plus Jack...

*TEDDY:*   *(laughs)* Yes, PLUS JACK...And that we can all be thinking of our lives in terms of National Peace and Personal Happiness...Thank you...

(AD LIB APPROVAL AND HAND CLAPPING)

*CLIFF:*   Short and sweet...Just like the girl who delivered it...

*TEDDY:*   You don't call five feet, three and a half SHORT, do you?

(LAUGHTER)

*CLIFF:*   Okay...At this point Margaret's going to sing to us again...Margaret, come a running...

*MARGARET:*   *(off little)* Okay, I'm coming...Hold my fruitcake Mommy...

*HAZEL:*   *(off little)* Oooh Goooeeey

(LAUGHTER)

*MARGARET:*   Okay Uncle Cliff...This time I'm going to sing Maresy-Dotz.

*CLIFF:*   Maresy-Dotz she says...Mom, you ready at the piano?...

*FANNY:*   *(off little)* Yes Clifford...

The cast in the studio, *(left to right)* Winifred Wolfe, Barton Yarborough, Announcer and Sound Effects men, Bernice Berwin, Michael Raffetto, Minetta Ellen, Page Gilman and J. Anthony Smythe. (1934)

*CLIFF:*   Then take it away...

(MARGARET SINGS WITH PIANO...MARESY-DOTZ)

(LAUGHTER AND APPLAUSE)

*HENRY:*   Eh?...Where in the world did you learn a song like that Margaret?

*MARGARET:*   Over the radio...

*HENRY:*   *(grunts)*...

*MARGARET:*   Didn't you like it?

*HENRY:*   I might have if I'd understood a word you said...What were you talking
—Chinese?

(LAUGHTER)

*CLIFF:*   Okay, and now we'll call on Hank...Come up here Hank...

(AD LIB STUFF FROM KIDS...)

*CLIFF:*   Quiet...Okay folks, meet the other Herbert twin...Henry Barbour Herbert

(COMMENT AND APPLAUSE)

*CLIFF:*   What are you going to do Hank?

*HANK:*   I'm gonna prove that Margaret's not the only one who can sing in our
family...

*CLIFF:*   The young man's going to sing...Go ahead, let's have it...

*HANK:*   Okay...*(clears throat) (sings)*
There was an old hen, who had a wooden leg
Best old hen that ever laid an egg...
Laid more eggs than any hen on the farm...
If she laid a little ham, wouldn't do any harm...

*BEN:*   *(laughs)* If she laid a little ham...*(laughs)*

(LAUGHTER)

*BEN:*   By-doggie, that KILLS me...

(LAUGHTER)

*CLIFF:*   Okay, and now I think we should hear from Dad...Come on up here Dad...

*HENRY:*   Yes, yes...

*CLIFF:*   *(coming to mike)* Introducing the Head of the House of Barbour, alias
Father Barbour, alias The GOVERNOR...

(LAUGHTER)

*HENRY:*   No Clifford...That's one thing NOBODY ever called me...The Governor...

*CLIFF:*   Okay Dad...The floor's yours...

*HENRY:*   Yes, yes...Thank you...Well, when Clifford asked me to say something this evening, I set about preparing a few notes...I think what I have to say is very pertinent to this day and age...This is it...

In these days with the gods of war abroad and the armies of vengeful hate on the march and with nations being swallowed up and boundary lines vanishing and states and institutions and personalities of power and position tumbling in a shower of unutterable chaos, and with the very foundations of civilization trembling on the very brink, it is only natural that each of us should be looking for something firm, something staunch, something honest to which we may cling. Something that neither fire, nor flood, nor earth tremors, nor avarice, nor greed, nor war, nor rumor of war can disturb or make insecure.

What IS that something?

In these United States we have the American family. So long as the American home shall live with its wholesomeness, with its ideals and its basic principles of discipline and citizenship, we have little to fear. But once let the family of this or any God-fearing nation lose its unity, its identity or its self-respect and the fate of Sodom and Gomorrah will be a small catastrophe indeed compared to the bitterness, the affliction and the desolation which will encompass that nation. Witness the plague that is upon Germany today; sense her inner desperation!

What has come upon her she would visit upon us also!

If the force of the enemy is to accomplish its stated purpose, which is the destruction of the democratic way of life and substitution of rule by fist and heel, then it must exterminate the very foundation of our civilization...The FAMILY! For so long as one American home is intact, there remains a living, growing root from which will stem a new force for freedom. In every wholesome family there is compressed all the idealism, all the functions, all the essentials of a democratic government!

It is in the family circle the child first learns the lessons of citizenship; where he first learns the social graces enabling him to live in peace and goodwill with his fellows; where he develops a feeling for truth and honor and is taught a sincere regard for his national and religious institutions; where he is given the fundamentals of freedom and equality and is taught the relationships which exist between honorable peoples.

Our enemies know this!

They know that the first thing they must do when they have invaded a freedom-loving country is to destroy the home; rip the family apart; kill or enslave the fathers; send the mothers to concentration camps or to factories and work farms; gather up the children and send them to institutions where their young minds may be wiped clean of democratic teachings.

That's what we're fighting against today! The madness of immoral and unprincipled leadership which is loose in Europe today! We're fighting against minds fixed on a single purpose; to destroy all humane civilization!

We are fighting FOR the privilege of keeping home and family intact; for the preservation of the sacred rites of marriage and for the very fundamental virtues on which honorable relationships between a man and a woman are built!

We are in arms to protect our native right to rear our children in the way we see fit; teach them the ideologies we ourselves were taught as children; teach them the prayers we love; teach them the graciousness of living; the beauties of goodness and truth; reveal to them the marvels of nature and the wonders accomplished by the mind and hand of man; show them the privileges of good citizenship and the heart-warming security to be found in a government of, for and by the people! All this without interference of any kind.

We are on the march to keep our home inviolate! To protect the precious right to close our door on the world; yes even against the world! To know that by written word in the Constitution of the United States we are guaranteed a privacy within our four walls which cannot be invaded. THIS is why we fight! For the root and the stem of a democratic way of life, which is the family! For that tiny compact unit of ideal government which is the home! The seed of ever-lasting freedom and deathless aggression against oppression!


(SINCERE AD LIB REACTION)

*TEDDY:*   Father Barbour, you wrote that yourself?

*HENRY:*   Yes, yes...

*HAZEL:*   Father I want a copy of that...

*HENRY:*   Eh?....

*HAZEL:*   I want to put that in my scrap book to read to my children as they grow older...I think children have got to be taught that the family is the ROOT OF CIVILIZATION...It's something too few people realize these days.

*HENRY:*   You're welcome to a copy...

*MARGARET:*   I liked it too, Grandfather.

*SKIPPY:*   Yeah, so did I...But it was kinda long, wasn't it?

(LAUGHTER)

*IRENE:*   Okay Mother Barbour, are you ready at the piano?

*FANNY:*   Yes, Irene...

*IRENE:*   Okay...Begin playing...

(PIANO...BEST BE THE TIE THAT BINDS)

*IRENE:*  *(on cue)* Come on...Everyone up on his feet...

(REACTION AND MURMUR)

*IRENE:*  Now join hands and sing...

(SINGING BEGINS WITH IRENE IN FOREGROUND OTHERS IN BACKGROUND)

(SLOWLY IRENE FADES BACK INTO SINGERS...THEN SLOWLY FADE UP ON MARGARET...THEN SHE DROPS BACK AND WHOLE GROUP FINISHES TOGETHER)

*IRENE:*  *(prayer)*
  The Lord watch between me and thee
  While we are absent one from another
  And bring us safely through yet another year...

*HENRY:*  *(softly)* Yes, yes...

*IRENE:*  Amen!

(ORGAN)

*ANN:*  In the spirit of the Barbours, let me also wax lyrical:
  Planned saving is a New Year MUST
  It isn't the dollars in the bank that rust!
  Victory Bonds don't fluctuate
  For each you own now get its mate.
  To spend as usual is a fatal error
  Building toward tomorrow's terror.
  Restraint is a virtue for every man
  Who is a responsible citizen.
  Plan your saving, plan your spending
  For future good things which are pending.
  Your war-time income and how you use it
  Is potent stuff! Please don't abuse it!

*ANN:*  Remember that! The stability of our United States currency depends on what you do with your war-time income! Save! Prevent inflation!

(ORGAN UP)

*ANN:*  You have just heard the 12th and final chapter of Book 52 of One Man's Family, a Carlton E. Morse drama written and produced for the makers of Fleischmann's Yeast. The opening Chapter of Book 53 will come to you next week at this same time.

# CHAPTER SIX

## The Extended "Family" Sponsors and Promotions

When "One Man's Family" went on the air in 1932, it was without the comfort of a backing sponsor. As with any new program, its survival depended upon audience response.

But its potential as an advertising vehicle was immense. New ground was then being broken in radio. For the first time, the medium was financially accessible to most people. And more importantly, coast-to-coast networking heralded a turning point in the history of culture: the ability to communicate a single event to vast numbers of people without regard to class or location. With nationwide broadcasting capacity came the powerful economics of nationally syndicated advertising.

Don Gillman, the NBC executive responsible for bringing "Family" onto the airwaves, was one of the visionaries who clearly saw the expanded possibilities of radio. He also had an intuitive faith in the right person at the right time. Carlton E. Morse did not do him injustice in this belief: "One Man's Family" soon joined a short list of programs rated by advertising agencies as notably having what it takes to inspire pay dirt, loyalty.

It wasn't until 1935, however, that the show picked up its first major sponsor, Standard Brands. Before then, it was carried by the network's sustaining advertising and the limited sponsorship of Wesson Oil.

NBC cancelled its deal with Wesson when the Penn Tobacco Company wanted to sponsor "Family" as a nationwide vehicle to advertise its Kentucky Winners cigarettes. But the association with Penn was nipped in the bud due to listener protest against the linking of cigarettes with the clean-living Barbour family.

Jack and Teddy in a promotional photo for Wesson Oil.

Standard Brands, after initially signing the usual 26 week broadcasting contract, went on to renew its commitment for an unprecedented 14 years. Backing 727 weekly broadcasts, they were the longest-running sponsor in the program's history. Standard Brands products represented in commercials and print advertisements included Tender Leaf Tea, Royal Pudding, Fleischmann's Yeast and V-8 Juice. Of these, Tender Leaf was the major product backed; new at the time, its rise to second place in the tea industry was directly attributable to the "Family."

After losing Standard Brands as the result of management changes in the company, the network asked listeners to send letters or postcards showing their support, to help attract a new sponsor. Sixty thousand pieces of mail arrived in a three-week period, and more followed.

In 1950, Miles Laboratories picked up the sponsorship, carrying it through 1954 and more than 1,000 daily broadcasts. Its advertised products included Alka-Seltzer, Bactine and One-a-Day Vitamins. Miles terminated its support in the belief that they had saturated the radio audience and it was time to move on to the new medium of television. Thereafter, until the last broadcast in 1959, various sponsors including Toni and RCA backed the show on a participating or sustaining basis.

Following industry practice, special premiums and promotional giveaways were offered throughout the life of the program, either by NBC or the sponsors. They ran the gamut from photographs of the cast to sheet music, "Family" scrapbooks, record albums and flower seed offers.

Most of these premiums contained thematic material from the show in the form of letters, prose, or poetry discussing love of country and family, individual responsibility and the process of growing up. References to the giveaways were sometimes worked into series broadcasts; thus, both the show and the premium reinforced the audience's interest in each other.

## Fanny Barbour

—"Mother" Barbour to her millions of admirers who listen to "One Man's Family," radio's most popular dramatic serial, on the N.B.C. Red Network every Wednesday night. Listen in!

*Mother Barbour says:*

# "My family would be lost without TENDER LEAF TEA"

"*I know that every mother and manager of a household has the same problems that I have—if not more. I wonder how many are trying to keep things running smoothly and everybody in a good humor, without the enormous help which comes from serving delicious tea?*

"*It may sound extravagant to say that Tender Leaf Tea is an 'enormous help,' but the soothing, calming, invigorating effect of this excellent tea is no figment of my imagination. We enjoy the flavor so much—but more than that, many of our most disturbing problems seem to solve themselves when the Barbour family gathers around for tea.*"

*Fanny Barbour*

# "The new TENDER LEAF TEA BALLS are wonderful!"

"*HELLO! . . . Oh, I'm so glad you called . . . No, I wasn't doing anything but having a cup of tea. I made it with one of the new Tender Leaf Tea Balls, and they're WONDERFUL . . . No, the tea is packed in a new kind of filter paper—the hot water FILTERS through it, so you get ALL the flavor and no stray tea leaves in your cup . . . You'll like Tender Leaf Tea better than ever—come on over and have a cup!*"

HAZEL BARBOUR—known to millions of radio fans who follow "One Man's Family," radio's most popular dramatic serial, on the N.B.C. Red Network Thursday nights—on Pacific Coast Red Network Stations Sunday nights.

NOW—every tea ball a tea FILTER! With Tender Leaf Tea Balls, you not only get the choice, young, TOP leaves of the tea plant—you get a new, superior method of making tea that is ALWAYS clear and sparkling—NEVER cloudy or speckled.

And the FLAVOR! It's the delicious full flavor of Tender Leaf Tea itself—no "foreign" taste. The filter paper is tasteless, odorless, insoluble in water.

Be the first in your neighborhood to serve tea made with the new *different* Tender Leaf Tea Balls. Your grocer has them 8 or 20 to the package. Also Tender Leaf Tea in 3½- and 7-oz. packages. Enjoy it today!

NOW, in buying tea at your grocer's, you can select the choice, young TOP leaves of the tea plant—leaves packed with the flavor and fragrance that make tea the world's most popular drink! Simply ask for "Tender Leaf Tea"—every package is filled with the choice, young tea leaves. No coarse, heavy leaves are included for bulk.

Your grocer has this special tea in 3½- and 7-oz. packages, and in tea balls. Call for "Tender Leaf Tea" by name—try it today!

The new Tender Leaf Tea Ball is a tea FILTER—no cloudiness or specks of tea in the cup.

Some of the "One Man's Family" premiums were notably elaborate examples of their genre. One of these was *Teddy's Diary*. Offered in 1937, the diary was 32 pages detailing in Teddy's childish hand the major events in her life the previous year. It also included a list of "good books to read," suggested by her father, Paul, and a letter from Father Henry to Jack upon his entering Stanford. More than 500,000 requests were received for this item. WOW!, I'm impressed!

# Diary

November 30, 1936

You know, Diary, the house next door belongs to Claudia. She rents it to people. But the last people moved out six months ago. And now it's an empty house.

This afternoon the queerest thing happened. Claudia and Cliff went over to inspect it because you have to do that to an empty house. And SOMEBODY locked them in a bedroom upstairs. They got out and the men folks went over and searched, but didn't find anything.

Dear Diary, do you believe in ghosts?

# Diary

December 1, 1936

They found Claudia's handkerchief in the empty house. Now Father Barbour thinks she's been meeting somebody over there. She says she hasn't, but she won't tell us what she DOES know.

Ooooooooh, but it's exciting.

December 2, 1936

More THRILLS! Today Jack told Father Barbour that HE was the ghost and the mysterious Mr. X over at the house next door. Jack has been meeting Betty Carter over there he says. He says he didn't know he was getting Claudia

# Diary

into trouble by not telling. If he knew that he would have told sooner. Father Barbour was ~~very~~ awful angry. He went to Betty's folks. They all decided Jack and Betty can't see each other for awhile.

December 7, 1936

Young folks have just GOT to snoop if they ever want to find out anything. Anyway, I heard Paul telling Cliff and Claud what Really happened in the 'house next door. Jack and Betty were keeping a man named Danny Frank over there. They were feeding him and everything. Danny Frank was an old sweetheart of

# Diary

Hazel's before she knew Bill. Jack and Betty thought it would be romantic to keep him over there so he could get a glimpse of Hazel without Hazel seeing him. Paul says nobody can tell Hazel or Father Barbour. It is liable to cause trouble. I don't understand why, but it is something about Hazel's past, or something, so we've got to keep it a secret, Diary.

December 18, 1936

goodness. EVERYTHING happened today. Jack and Betty eloped to Reno in an auto. Paul and Father Barbour and Mr. Carter went after them in one of Paul's airplanes and brought them home. Jack was going to leave home. But Hazel and the others talked to him for a

# Diary

a long time. And finally Jack went down in the garden to Father Barbour. Pretty soon everything was straightened out. Paul says it was all on account of a wonderful letter Father Barbour wrote. Paul says he will let

me read ~~the~~ the letter sometime and maybe even keep a copy of it. Anyways, I like Father Barbour and here is his picture.

Jan. 5, 1937
A new family moved in the empty house next door. It's Professor Stephen Waite and his daughter Ann. She's twenty and she is awfully nice and she plays the piano better than ANYBODY. And she sings too. Professor Waite teaches music.

# Diary

Dear grandchildren. This Diary
is for you. Here is Paul's
picture of me the way I
am going to look when I
am your grandmother
Your friend,
Teddy.

*The Barbour Family Scrapbook* contained 18 pages of family photographs and fictional newspaper clippings. Offered in 1951, over 235,000 copies of this "photo album" were sent out. *Mother Barbour's Favorite Recipes* was created as a souvenir of the show's 20th anniversary. Woven through the collection of recipes, photos and vignettes was a long letter from Mother Fanny recounting the family history from her perspective and in exhaustiive detail. More than 230,000 copies were requested when it was published and 10 years later people were still asking for copies.

The last premium offered on the program was *This I Give: Father Barbour's Holographic Will & Memory Book*. A 32-page album, it had the most pictures of any of the premium books, and again traced the family's saga from the beginning. Two hundred sixty thousand copies were sent out to listeners.

All these premiums helped to make the Barbour family that much more real. The attention to detail that went into fleshing out the picture of a wholesome American family with photos and memorabilia was not lost on a large segment of Americans.

# CHAPTER SEVEN

## Lieutenant Jack Barbour Leaves for the Pacific

Before turning to the opening chapter of this new book concerning the lives of the Barbours, we come to the inevitable Author's Preface, which on this occasion is particularly significant.

"The new book concerning the lives of the Barbour clan, which we open this month of April, has twofold significance. First, it is the 50th full-length, hundred-thousand-word novel about this San Francisco family. Already, fifty times a hundred thousand words, or five million words, have been written about Henry and Fanny Barbour and their offspring to the second and third generations. And still the story has not been told.

The second important fact about this month of April, 1944, is our anniversary. This month "One Man's Family" begins its 13th consecutive year on the air. And in this matter I would like to pay special tribute to those veteran personalities of radio who, through their loyalty and continued service, have helped to build and sustain the quality and character of this radio program.

Those who have been with us from the very first broadcast back in April, 1932 are: J. Anthony Smythe, who plays the character of Father Barbour; Minetta Ellen, who is Mother Barbour; Michael Raffetto, who is Paul Barbour; Bernice Berwin, who is Hazel Barbour Herbert; Barton Yarborough, who is Clifford; and Page Gilman, who is Jack.

In the case of this last, Page is in fact Second Lieutenant Gilman, at the moment stationed at the Field Artillery Officers Training School at Fort Sill, Oklahoma.

When the war is won, he will return to take up his role as head of the second-generation house of Barbour, along with Betty.

There is one other who has been with us continually from the first broadcast. This is our organist, Paul Carson. Not only has he given us our musical background for 12 years, but he is the creator of our theme music, "Patricia," which recently has been published and just now has been released to music stores throughout the nation.

And then there's Winifred Wolf who has played the role of Teddy for 11 years, and Jean Rouverol, who has been Jack's wife, Betty, for seven years. These are the people who have interpreted the words, ideas and moods of the scripts that have come over the air to you week after week, month after month, year after year. And it is my hope that this same group of friendly personalities, along with the new generation that is becoming articulate, will continue to carry on the saga of one certain American family for many years to come."

Carlton E. Morse

# ANNOUNCEMENTS AND DESCRIPTIONS
## FOR
## ONE MAN'S FAMILY
## CHAPTER NINE – BOOK FIFTY-FOUR

### "LIEUT. JACK BARBOUR LEAVES FOR THE PACIFIC"

| | | |
|---|---|---|
| **Tuesday** | **4:30-5:00 p.m.** | **May 29, 1945** |
| **Tuesday** | **7:30-8:00 p.m.** | **May 29, 1945** |

*ANNOUNCER:*  One Man's Family, brought to you by the makers of Royal Desserts and Tender Leaf Tea.

(ORGAN)

*ANN:*  One Man's Family is dedicated to the Mothers and Fathers of the younger generation and to their bewildering offspring. Tonight we present Chapter Nine, Book Fifty-four entitled:

(ORGAN)

*ANN:*  "LIEUT. JACK BARBOUR LEAVES FOR THE PACIFIC!"

(ORGAN)

*ANN:*  There comes a time in every show, when the best way to tell a story is to let the audience behind the scenes. And I think this is one of those times. As those of you who have listened to One Man's Family throughout the years know, the character of Jack Barbour is played by Page Gilman, now Lieut. Page Gilman of the United States Army Field Artillery. That is why the character of Jack has been in the show so infrequently the last two years. Because Lieut. Gilman has been stationed at Fort Sill, Oklahoma...Just as Jack Barbour has been at Fort Sill all these months. And now suddenly everything is changed! Lieut. Gilman is being shipped out to the Pacific. He is home on leave this week and that makes it possible for us to have the character home with the family one more time before he takes up his military duties on the other side of the world. Lieut. Gilman was thirteen years old when he first came into One Man's Family. That was 13 years ago, and believe me when I say that to us on the show, his going away is the same as sending out our own son and brother. That is the story behind the story of tonight's broadcast. But now the show!

When Lieut. Jack Barbour suddenly dropped in on his family night before last and said he was headed for active duty in the Pacific, and that he had just 48 hours leave, his family closed in about him like the arms of a mother about a small child. The desire to do something for him, to BE something to him; to help sustain him in preparation for this new adventure was overwhelming. But as the hours went by and they found him relaxed, cheerful, confident, everyone else began to relax and the household was back to normal again. And now it's time for him to go...Almost time! An Army jeep is to pick him up in front of the house at 4:30...It's 4:10 now...In the last 20 minutes at home, he's trying to have a little private conversation with each member of his family. Just at the moment, he's up in his Mother's sewing room with her.

*JACK:*   It's too bad Cliff and Irene couldn't get down from the Sky Ranch today...

*FANNY:*   Skippy's got the influenza...

*JACK:*   Oh sure...I said goodbye to them last night when they were here. It's okay...

*FANNY:*   Where's Betty?

*JACK:*   (*amused*) She's in the nursery prettying up the three daughters...She says she wants my last glimpse of my family to be something extra special...

*FANNY:*   Betty's a good wife Jack...

*JACK:*   (*sober*) Yeah...

*FANNY:*   A devoted wife and a good daughter-in-law...

*JACK:*   (*anxiously*) It's working out alright having her and the children here with you and Dad?

*FANNY:*   It would be a very lonesome house without her...

*JACK:*   I'm glad you feel that way...Uh...Mom, about my going out to the Pacific...

*FANNY:*   Yes, Jack...

*JACK:*   (*amused*) What's that you're doing?

*FANNY:*   Just a little needle work...

*JACK:*   (*amused*) What you used to call 'fancy work'?

*FANNY:*   (*amused*) Yes...

*JACK:*   Well, what I started to say is...You can be very comfortable about it because its the thing I want to do most...

*FANNY:*   Yes, I know...

*JACK:*   I'm going out to do something I know how to do and I'm confident I can do it well...It's cost the Government between $20,000 and $25,000 to educate me to do the job...Out of sheer desire to prove that I'm now capable of functioning as I've been trained, I want to go.

*FANNY:*   Yes my dear...

*JACK:*   Maybe you think it's reckless and unthinking to look at it that way...Maybe you think I'm not considering Betty and the children enough...

*FANNY:*   No Jack, I don't think that.

*JACK:*   Oh...I...I rather expected you would...

*FANNY:*   No son, because if you DIDN'T feel the way you do, who would there be to fight the war? If young men your age didn't have that outlook, this nation would be in a sorry fix today.

*JACK:*   Mom, you're amazing...

*FANNY:*   Am I?

*JACK:*   You know, it's funny...You were the one I...I rather dreaded to talk with alone...

*FANNY:*   I understand my dear...Mother's getting old...Mother hasn't got very good control of her emotions anymore...Mother will cling to me and cry and I won't be able to stand it...

*JACK:*   *(softly)* You're WONDERFUL Mom...

*FANNY:*   You'll be gone a year...two years...maybe even three years...

*JACK:*   *(gently)* Yes...

*FANNY:*   Your father and I won't be getting any younger...

*JACK:*   But you'll be here when I get back...

*FANNY:*   I hope so...

*JACK:*   You will...ALL of you...I want everything just as it is, when I come back...

*FANNY:*   We'll try to keep it that way...And now hadn't you better go talk to your father? See what time it is...

*JACK:*   I expect I had...Don't get up...Just put your face up here...

(PAUSE)

*FANNY:*   *(starts to cry)*

*JACK:*   *(softly)* Mother...Mother...You mustn't.

(ORGAN THEME)

*HAZEL:*   *(off little)* Oh there you are...

*JACK:*   Hello Hazel...

*HAZEL:*   I was just coming upstairs to find you...Where's Mother?

*JACK:* She went to her room...

*HAZEL:* You said goodbye to her?

*JACK:* Yes...Here, let's sit down here on the steps for a minute.

*HAZEL:* Have you time?

*JACK:* Sure...I was going down to see Dad in the library, but I'd rather talk to you first...Sit down.

*HAZEL:* *(amused)* A little confidential chat on the stair landing, huh...

*JACK:* Yeah...You know Hazel, it's queer, but it seems like I want to talk about some different phase of my...my life with each member of the family...What comes into my mind isn't anything like what I said to Mom...

*HAZEL:* Yes, I understand that.

*JACK:* I keep thinking of when I was a kid, sitting here with you...I remember how I used to get in your hair and Claudia's whenever you had boys around...I must have been obnoxious as all get out.

*HAZEL:* *(laughs)* Well you had your moments, I'll give you that...

*JACK:* I remember how you married Bill Herbert and how Nicky Lacey followed Claudia back here from England and how Dad disliked him at first.

*HAZEL:* Oh but he got to like Nicky among his favorite people...

*JACK:* Sure...And those wonderful summers up at the Sky Ranch...You're all going up again THIS summer, aren't you?

*HAZEL:* It looks like it.

*JACK:* Yeah...And think where I'll be...

*HAZEL:* *(sober)* Yes, I am...

*JACK:* China, India, Burma, Manchuria...*(shrugs)* Who knows...

*HAZEL:* We'll be thinking a great deal about you, all the months you're away...

*JACK:* *(amused)* You know I just thought of something...

*HAZEL:* What's that?

*JACK:* *(amused)* Did you know I named your twins?

*HAZEL:* Hank and Pinky?

*JACK:* *(amused)* Sure...Almost the day they were born...Paul took me to the hospital to see them and there they were...One of them looked exactly like Dad...

*HAZEL:* *(amused)* Oh no...

*JACK:* Sure he did...So I told Paul he'd have to be Henry after his grandfather... Hank for short...

*HAZEL:* *(laughs)* And Pinky was SOOO redheaded...

*JACK:* *(amused)* And there hasn't been a redhead in the Barbour family for GEN-ERATIONS...

*HAZEL:* *(laughs)* *(sobers)* Jack...

*JACK:* Yeah?

*HAZEL:* You'll keep the letters coming, won't you?

*JACK:* Hey, I've done pretty good at Fort Sill...

*HAZEL:* Yes, but this is going to be different...Keep them coming twice a week, especially on Betty and Mother's account...

*JACK:* Yes, but they'll have to remember the mail facilities out there...

*HAZEL:* Oh yes...But you do your part, and we'll do ours.

*JACK:* It's a deal.

*HAZEL:* *(amused)* Jack do you remember the time you rented a set of full tails about ten times too big for you and went to pay a call on your heart's desire...?

*JACK:* Oh boy...I was 13...

*HAZEL:* *(amused)* And she slammed the door in your face...She thought you were clowning.

*JACK:* *(amused)* Busted my heart wide open...Hey, you know something?

*HAZEL:* What?

*JACK:* Put things like that in your letters...They help...

*HAZEL:* Recollections of our family life...

*JACK:* Yeah...Things like that in a letter get a fellow's train of thought to working ...Take his mind off what's happening at the moment.

*HAZEL:* A good idea...I'll do it.

*JACK:* *(reluctant)* Well, time's getting short...

*HAZEL:* Of course it is...I've kept you longer than I meant...

*JACK:* No, it's just that I've still got to see Dad and Paul and Teddy, and I want to get back up to Betty before the Jeep gives me the beep-beep.

*HAZEL:* Naturally...

*JACK:* Here, give me your hand...

*HAZEL:* You go ahead...I'll go up and talk to mother a little...

*JACK:* Hey, how about a kiss...

*HAZEL:* *(gently)* Of course...*(pause)* A girl's very proud and happy to have a brother like you, my dear.

*JACK:* *(softly)* See you after Tokyo...

*HAZEL:* *(near tears)* Yes...Go on now...

*JACK:* *(understanding)* Yeah...

(SOUND OF FOOTSTEPS FADING ON CARPETED STAIRS)

*HAZEL:* *(on cue)* *(to self)* After Tokyo *(leaving mike)* and the earth has been cleansed of its madness...

(PAUSE)

*HENRY:* Eh?...Is that you Jack?

*JACK:* *(coming to mike)* Yeah, I just been saying goodbye to Mom and Hazel...

*HENRY:* So soon?

*JACK:* Yes, they'll be dropping by for me in about fifteen minutes...

*HENRY:* So seldom you're with us...So soon you go.

*JACK:* *(cheerful)* Dad you know I'm going to get a great pleasure out of two mental pictures of you.

*HENRY:* Eh?

*JACK:* One of them's sitting here in that big chair before the fire...

*HENRY:* Yes, yes...

*JACK:* The other is of you out in the garden on your knees...

*HENRY:* *(agrees)* Typical, I expect...

*JACK:* Yeah...

*HENRY:*  Er…

*JACK:*  Huh?

*HENRY:*  *(hastily)* Nothing, nothing…

*JACK:*  Yeah…

(PAUSE)

*HENRY:*  *(on cue)* Eh?…What's the matter here anyway? The minutes are slipping by and we're not saying anything to each other…

*JACK:*  Funny, too, because I was full of things I wanted to talk to you about and now I can't remember any of them.

*HENRY:*  Stage fright…That's what's the matter with us, stage fright…Our moment's HERE and we're tongue-tied.

*JACK:*  Well, it IS a pretty big thing to try to put into words all the love and affection and appreciation a son has for his father…

*HENRY:*  Eh? You feel that way?

*JACK:*  Dad I never appreciated the kind of home you created for us here in Sea Cliff until I got out into the Army and had a look at some of the rest of the world…

*HENRY:*  I like hearing you say that Jack…I'll remember those words and keep them with me.

*JACK:*  Well, they're TRUE words…

*HENRY:*  Yes, yes…They'll be a great comfort to me…

*JACK:*  When I see how a lot of kids are turned out on the world by their homes without any preparation; without any knowledge of good citizenship and human decency…Yeah, right here in the United States, people are growing up into misfits, incompetents and men and women with criminal tendencies, just simply because they didn't have an adequate homelife or parents with a grain of common sense. The Army's FULL of guys like that.

*HENRY:*  *(pleased)* Well then, I don't need to convert YOU to the idea that the Family is the keystone to good government…

*JACK:*  Not me…

*HENRY:*  Eh? You've got ten minutes more in our midst and we're talking about social problems…What's got into me anyway?

*JACK:*  Maybe it's hard for us to say what's inside of us…Maybe we're just talking around the bush because the 'REAL' things just won't come out.

*HENRY:* Yes, yes...Before you came in I was sitting here thinking of you...Trying to make out what there was in your life which had brought you to this point in your life.

*JACK:* What circumstances have arranged it so that I'm about to jump off the Western Hemisphere and land on a battle front some nine or ten thousand miles from here?

*HENRY:* Yes, yes...

*JACK:* I don't know, Dad...

*HENRY:* You weren't such an exceptional baby...

*JACK:* *(protests, amused)* Hey...!

*HENRY:* No, you weren't...You gurgled and you hiccoughed and you cried your full share...I'm sure there wasn't anything in your infancy which pointed out that you were to become a Second Lieutenant in the Field Artillery...

*JACK:* *(amused)* I wouldn't know...

*HENRY:* And in your boyhood and adolescence, I don't recall anything...Yes, the policeman on the block brought you home by the ear a couple of times for pranks...But he did the same to other boys...There was nothing in the little boy who said his prayers or the adolescent who suffered so much from calf-love, to indicate you were going to grow into a man of war...

*JACK:* In fact, if any boy was taught 'peace at any price' it was me...When Paul came back from the last war with a bad leg and shell shock, the very word 'war' was taboo in this house.

*HENRY:* And I'm sure there was nothing in your study of law at Stanford nor in your marriage and production of three daughters which points you out as a belligerent fellow.

*JACK:* Well it just goes to show Dad...You can raise a man to peace and good will, but if you push him around enough he's still going to develop into a fighter.

*HENRY:* *(grunts)* I'm going to say goodbye to you here in the house...I don't want to see you drive away...

*JACK:* *(agrees)* Nobody's going out...

*HENRY:* I just can't bear to see people get into automobiles and drive out of my life...I...something tears loose inside of me every time it happens...

*JACK:* *(softly)* I know...

*HENRY:* *(sudden energy)* Well, I think I'll get up...*(grunts)*...I see Margaret outside...I think I'll go down in the garden with her until you're gone...

*JACK:* Sure, if you want to...

HENRY: *(near tears)* If I put my arm around you…If I touch you…

JACK: Okay Dad…I understand…

HENRY: God Bless you, boy…*(leaving mike)* God Bless you.

JACK: *(up)* You too, Dad!

*I'm tearing up as I read this fine passage on April 9, 1997. MLP*

(PAUSE)


JACK: *(sighs) (to self)* Well, that's life as she's lived today, I guess.

TEDDY: Hey, you in here by yourself?

JACK: Oh hello, Teddy…

TEDDY: I thought you were here with Father Barbour.

JACK: We just said goodbye…He's gone down into the garden…

TEDDY: Oh…I was going to tip-toe by and not bother and then I saw you standing here alone…

JACK: *(admiring)* You know something Teddy…

TEDDY: What?

JACK: You've got to be one of the best doggone looking girls I know…

TEDDY: Oooh…

JACK: You think I'm kidding…I mean it…I'll bet you're number one priority with the boys in the hospital…

TEDDY: *(amused)* So the Army's giving you a 'way with the girls,' is that it?

JACK: I've ALWAYS had a way with the one girl I cared about…

TEDDY: Betty?

JACK: Who else?

TEDDY: She said she wasn't going outside to see you leave…

JACK: No, I'm going to say goodbye to her upstairs in her room…That's the easiest and the best…I'm saving her for last…

TEDDY: *(amused)* Naturally.

JACK: Teddy, what do you ever hear of Wayne Grubb and Tracey Baker…

*TEDDY:* Well you knew that Tracey was flying a P-38 and was shot down in the African campaign...He was in the hospital for a little and then he went to flying a bomber over Germany.

*JACK:* Not a scratch, huh?

*TEDDY:* No, and the last letter said he was being transferred to the Pacific theater...

*JACK:* Tracey's turned out to be quite a lad...Is he still in love with you?

*TEDDY:* We write regularly, but they aren't those kind of letters.

*JACK:* And Wayne Grubb?

*TEDDY:* Wayne's kind of gone out of my life; I hear maybe once every three months...He's in Supply...Last letter said he might get to Manila...

*JACK:* Then I might see him over there...

*TEDDY:* Uh huh...

*JACK:* *(amused)* Why do you say it like that?

*TEDDY:* I don't know...I was just thinking...I suppose they wouldn't be taking you if they didn't need you...

*JACK:* *(amused)* I doubt it...Why?

*TEDDY:* I...I guess I keep thinking of things from a nurse's point of view...

*JACK:* Oh...Oh yeah...

*TEDDY:* You've got a wonderful physique...And you've got a lot to live for when you come back...

*JACK:* In other words, take care of myself...

*TEDDY:* It's silly because like everyone else, you'll do what's required of you, but don't be careless...You'd be surprised what percentage of soldiers are in that hospital out there because they didn't do all they could to protect themselves...

*JACK:* I've been trained for that...

*TEDDY:* So were they, but some of them relaxed or forgot or just didn't GIVE A HOOT...And look at them now...And it wasn't necessary at all.

*JACK:* Yeah...

*TEDDY:* So that's what I mean when I say take care of yourself...Go out and give them all you got but play them close to your chest.

*JACK:* (*amused*) And this is the girl who was running around in pigtails five, six years ago...

*TEDDY:* You grow up fast in this day and age...

*JACK:* Yeah...

*TEDDY:* I'm on my way to the hospital now...I mustn't be late...

*JACK:* Okay, I'll go to the front door with you...

*TEDDY:* Alright...(*leaving mike*) It's hard to realize this is happening to you...

*JACK:* (*coming to mike*) I guess every man called overseas said the same thing.

(DOOR OPENS)

*TEDDY:* Well...see you when it's over.

*JACK:* Hey, do I have to ASK for kisses around here?

*TEDDY:* (*near tears*) I was hoping to get away fast...I'm not used to kissing the boys goodbye...(*pause*) There...Now let me go...

*JACK:* (*up little*) Yeah Teddy...See you when it's over.

(PAUSES...DOOR CLOSES)

*JACK:* (*to self*) Yeah...See you when it's over.

*PAUL:* (*off*) Oh Jack...

*JACK:* (*off little*) Oh hello Paul...(*coming to mike*) I thought you were probably up in your studio...

*PAUL:* (*fade in*) No, I've been waiting for you in the living room...

*JACK:* You know, this is the queerest experience of all of it...Trying to square accounts with everyone before I have to go.

*PAUL:* Having much success?

*JACK:* No.

*PAUL:* I thought not...

*JACK:* I don't know what's the matter...I don't seem to be able to say anything important...Everything's trivial...There's so much that ought to be said...So much I'd like Mom and Dad and all of you to know before I go, and I haven't said any of it...

*PAUL:* Of course...

The Barbour Family at home *(left to right)* Mother Barbour, Hazel, Paul, Jack, Clifford, Claudia, and Father Barbour.

*JACK:*  You...you really aren't surprised?

*PAUL:*  How can a man put into words what he feels towards those who created him and molded him and watched over him...He can't...Any more than the human creature can express himself eloquently to his God. What do people do when they want to thank their God or beseech his help...They sing homely, conventional hymns; they say simple often-repeated prayers; they get down on their knees and bow their heads in simple supplication; they give money to charity...All simple, homely, everyday words and gestures that have been said and done since the beginning of time. Do you think these things are the ACTUAL relationship between man and his Maker?...Not at all. They're only symbols! Man is too inarticulate to express the deep things of his mind and emotion. There just aren't words for them.

*JACK:*  But...but I flounder so...

*PAUL:*  Do you doubt that God knows our intent when we kneel? Of course not... And in just the same way Dad and Mom know the feeling in your heart when you look into their faces...Touch their hands...

*JACK:*  Then...then I'm NOT falling down...

*PAUL:*  Not at all...

*JACK:*  I...I've never heard you talk of God before, Paul...

*PAUL:*  I'm doing it purposely...When a man's going out where you may be going, God's a mighty important part of your life. A lot of the men don't take him with them, but those who do are comforted the most at difficult times.

*JACK:*  *(embarrassed)* I...I don't know whether I can or not...

*PAUL:*  It's not something to worry about...I just thought you'd like to know that when I was in France in the First World War I found there were times when I could talk to God when I couldn't talk with anyone else. I don't know who or what God is any more than you do, and I'm afraid my conception of him is pretty unorthodox and unconventional...I can't go with you where you're going...I just thought I'd like to give you something to think about if you ever get in a tight place...

*JACK:*  *(subdued)* Yeah...Thanks...

*PAUL:*  One other thing...Don't worry about Betty and the children...They'll get attention from all of us.

*JACK:*  I know that...Uh...There's something else though...

*PAUL:*  Let's have it...

*JACK:*  It's about myself.

*PAUL:*  Oh...

*JACK:*   Paul, you went through the last war…You must have some way of measuring a man…I mean…Well, do you think I can take care of the job ahead of me?

*PAUL:*   You'll have to find that answer inside yourself when the time comes.

*JACK:*   It…it's not something you can help me with?

*PAUL:*   I will say this, I've never known a good soldier yet who wasn't more afraid of BEING afraid than he was of actual combat.

*JACK:*   Yeah…Yeah we've talked about that a lot…I mean bull sessions and it's even had some official recognition…But I have a queer kind of sensation of being inadequate…Of wondering if my superior officers know my weaknesses… Afraid I'll be asked to do the ONE thing I won't be able to do…

*PAUL:*   What one thing?

*JACK:*   I don't know…But I'm sure there is something…

*PAUL:*   *(amused)* You've got a large, oversized dose of stage fright…

*JACK:*   *(amused)* Dad said he and I had stage fright was the reason we couldn't talk to each other…

*PAUL:*   It's still because you're ten thousand miles from action…Once you get your feet on the ground and begin going through all the routine you've acquainted yourself with in training camps, all that doubt and wonder will slip away…

*JACK:*   You know Paul, it just came to me…It's pretty doggone interesting isn't it…A soldier of 1918 talking to a soldier of 1945…And us being brothers…

*PAUL:*   *(agrees)* The old and the new…

*JACK:*   Were you eager to go to France in the last war?

*PAUL:*   Yes, of course.

*JACK:*   Just as I want to go to the Pacific?…I mean was there a feeling that if you didn't get to go you'd loose something out of your life?

*PAUL:*   Is that the way you feel?

*JACK:*   Yes…I've got Betty and the three children…If I don't go out into the world right now and do all the things men do, the opportunity will be gone and lost to me forever.

*PAUL:*   You feel it would be such a great loss…Never to have experienced active combat?

*JACK:*   It's more than the fighting, Paul…It's going places…experiencing things… finding out for yourself the color and texture and bigness of the world we're in…

*PAUL:*  I get it…

*JACK:*  The way you say that, I wonder if you DO?

*PAUL:*  Yes…You have suddenly come to realize you are a married man with three daughters…You suddenly see domestic duties facing you for the rest of your life…You're army career is giving you one last, glorious fling before you settle down to practicing law and becoming a staid family man.

*JACK:*  Is that the way you see it?

*PAUL:*  There's no use trying to be dishonest at this stage of the game…You've got only five or ten minutes longer and you'll be away from us one, maybe two, maybe three years…There's no use being anything but understanding and sympathetic at this late hour.

*JACK:*  *(hesitates)* I…I don't know Paul…Maybe that IS why I want to go…I'd never consciously thought of it that way…Maybe I DO want to store up adventure and action and excitement…Maybe so…I don't know why…

*PAUL:*  For your memories to feed on in the years to come when you're completely domesticated…

*JACK:*  I couldn't prevent myself from going if I WANTED to, but do you think I'm being disloyal to Betty for being anxious to go?

*PAUL:*  No.

*JACK:*  Because I DO want to come back to her and I don't know anybody who's crazier about his children…

*PAUL:*  You don't have to justify yourself to me.

*JACK:*  But it's confusing in my own mind…I think and dream about Betty and the children all the time I'm away from them…And yet here I'm anxious to go to the Pacific…It kinda hurts my conscience…

*PAUL:*  I wouldn't worry about it too much.

*JACK:*  I'm…I'm telling you these things because I just couldn't say it to anyone else…How could the folks or Betty understand…They'd think right away that I wasn't loyal…That I was losing interest in Betty…

*PAUL:*  Don't make too much of it.

*JACK:*  Huh?

*PAUL:*  It isn't important unless you make it so in your own mind…It simply boils down to the fact that you've been ordered to the Pacific Theater…You're glad of it…That's all there is to it.

*JACK:*  Doggone my conscience anyway…

*PAUL:* *(agrees)* The Barbours all have them…They can be very inconvenient…By the way, it's twenty-five after four.

*JACK:* Hey…

*PAUL:* That's only going to give you five minutes with Betty…

*JACK:* We decided we didn't want too long…It would just make it harder…That's why I saved Betty for last…So I could run down and get in the jeep and be gone the minute it arrived…You'll excuse me now?

*PAUL:* If you're going to dash out that fast, I'd better say goodbye now…

*JACK:* Yeah, I wish you would…No last minute stuff…

*PAUL:* Well, try to remember some of the things I've tried to say to you…Remember there's safety and security waiting for you when you come back to us…And above all don't worry about Betty.

*JACK:* Thank you Paul…

*PAUL:* Well…Goodbye…

*JACK:* Bye Paul…

(PAUSE)

*PAUL:* Well go on…go on…Betty's waiting…

*JACK:* Yeah, I…you bet…*(leaving mike)* See you when it's all over.

(SOUND OF FOOTSTEPS RUNNING UP STEPS OUT OF PICTURE)

(THEN FADE STEPS BACK IN TO FULL MIKE…STOP ON CUE)

(PAUSE)

(TAPPING ON DOOR)

*BETTY:* *(off)* Hello?

*JACK:* It's me Betty…

(DOOR OPENS)

*BETTY:* *(coming to mike)* *(fearful)* Is it time…Is it time yet?

*JACK:* *(exclaims)* Betty you're BEAUTIFUL…

*BETTY:* *(eager)* You like it?

*JACK:* I didn't know you had a dress like that…And what've you done to your hair…?

*BETTY:* Well I dolled the infant daughters all up and then I thought maybe you'd like to see ME looking beautiful too...

*JACK:* *(impressed)* Just a minute while I close the door...

(DOOR CLOSES)

*JACK:* Now come here and get yourself kissed...

*BETTY:* *(breathes)* Oh yes...

(PAUSE)

*JACK:* *(tender)* There...

*BETTY:* *(fearful)* It's almost time now, isn't it...

*JACK:* Almost...

*BETTY:* Have...have you said goodbye to everyone else?

*JACK:* Yep...Saved you for dessert...

*BETTY:* *(regretful)* I'm afraid your daughters are all asleep...Here they are over here.

*JACK:* *(amused)* *(coming to mike)* Maybe it's better that way...

*BETTY:* Maybe I should wake Elizabeth Sharon Ann, anyway...

*JACK:* No, don't...*(amused)* All washed and combed and curled...You know something Betty?

*BETTY:* What?

*JACK:* We're a pretty lucky couple...

*BETTY:* Oh yes...

*JACK:* Just shot full of luck, us Jack Barbours...

*BETTY:* *(uneasy)* Jack, we shouldn't brag about it...

*JACK:* Why not? It isn't every man who has the most beautiful wife in the world PLUS the three most beautiful daughters...

*BETTY:* *(uneasy)* But you're leaving us...

*JACK:* Just for a little...I'll be back in no time at all...Look, already men are coming home from war...They've been out fighting and now their time is up and they're coming home.

*BETTY:* I...I wish YOU were coming back instead of just going out.

JACK: *(protests)* But think of the interesting letters I'm going to send you from all the interesting places...

BETTY: Is that going to be as good as somebody to lie close to...Somebody to put his arms around me...Is that as good?

JACK: *(tender)* Darling...We had it all figured out, remember...No last minute being sorry for ourselves...

BETTY: *(near tears)* But keep your arm around me...You can do that until it's time...

JACK: Of course I can...

BETTY: Oh Jack, make it all happen quickly...Make it so that you can come back for always and I can feel complete and whole again...Not just HALF a thing getting along...

JACK: As quickly as I can, Betty...

BETTY: *(eager, soft)* And then we'll live like a real American family should live, again...I'll cook your breakfast in the morning and you'll read the paper and go down to your law office, and I'll have the whole day to teach our children OUR way of life and have the house ready for your homecoming...And after dinner, we can be alone to plan our plans or go over to Mother and Father Barbours or go to a show...Everything will be so safe and sure and wonderful again...

JACK: It will, won't it...

BETTY: Make it happen, Jack...Make it come true...

JACK: *(softly)* That's my going away promise to you...

BETTY: *(eager)* It IS?

JACK: To come back and fit into OUR way of life...That's my promise.

BETTY: *(softly)* Oh YES...

(TAPPING ON DOOR)

TEDDY: *(off)* Jack...

JACK: Yes Teddy?

TEDDY: *(off)* The Jeep is down in front...

BETTY: *(softly)* Oh no, Jack...

JACK: Betty, you mustn't hang onto me...You mustn't make it so hard...

BETTY: *(softly)* Not this time, Jack...Don't go this time...

*JACK:* *(softly)* Darling, they're waiting...Let me go quickly, the way I wanted to...*(effort)* That's it...Goodbye, darling...

(DOOR OPENS)

*JACK:* Please don't look that way...Just say goodbye...

*BETTY:* *(low)* Of course...Goodbye, darling...

(PAUSE)

(DOOR CLOSES)

*BETTY:* *(tears)* I wish I'd been braver...*(whispers)* I wish I'd been braver!

(ORGAN)

*ANN:* You have just heard Chapter Nine, Book Fifty-Four of One Man's Family, written and produced by Carlton E. Morse for the makers of Royal Desserts and Tender Leaf Tea. Chapter Ten, entitled "WHAT TOOK PAUL TO WASHINGTON" will come to you next week at this same time.

# CHAPTER EIGHT

# Two Good Memories

Many years ago a letter came to me from a southern state prison, signed not by name, but with a convict number. I have not thought of that letter for almost three decades until this morning. I was down in the lower garden cutting out the old canes of the blackberry vines and twining the vigorous, young tendrils about the supporting wires.

It always has been a marvel to me, and a sense of satisfaction, how a mind wanders and strays into other years and faraway places, among long forgotten events, when the hands are busy in or about the garden soil. There is something of earth and earthy toil which is soothing to a defensive, uneasy mind. This happy lassitude appeals to me as Nature's own sedative; a day-dreaming relaxation very near the level of sleep itself.

It was in this pleasant euphoria that the convict's letter floated into my consciousness. I still have the original in one of the old scrap books, but there is no need for it. I know its message by heart.

He wrote in a childish awkward hand :

> "I am an old man now. I have been here many, many years, having been convicted in my youth of murder and sentenced to life imprisonment. I was raised in an orphanage and know nothing of my mother or father. I did not know there were parents such as Mother and Father Barbour and I did not know there were families such as the Barbour family. If I had known, I would never be in this prison now. Just recently they have put a radio in my cell block and one of the shows we are allowed to hear is One Man's Family, on Sunday evening. *(EDITOR'S NOTE: One Man's Family was on the NBC Network on Sunday evenings for many years until Mr. Morse went to New York to translate the show into a three-year television*

*drama.)* This is my favorite show and the Barbours are my family. I have adopted them."

Thus wrote convict No. 8865646. As I snipped the old growth, tied the new and sucked on a finger gouged by a blackberry briar, my mind dredged up still another old letter. This one from a judge of the Chicago Juvenile Courts, asking for a certified, as-broadcast copy of the previous week's "Family" episode. A black youth had been picked up and identified as a purse snatcher. He alleged he had been at home listening to *One Man's Family,* and could give an outline of the entire show. The script was sent and the young man acquitted himself handsomely and was released.

Ten years passed. There came into my office in Hollywood a black Los Angeles policeman and with him was his brother in the uniform of the United States Marines, just home from fighting in the South Pacific. The young veteran was the youth who had saved himself by knowing the "One Man's Family" script so thoroughly. He and his brother had come to thank me and the show for helping to keep him out of jail.

# CHAPTER NINE

## The Rededication of Nicky

ANNOUNCEMENTS AND DESCRIPTIONS
FOR
ONE MAN'S FAMILY
CHAPTER FOUR – BOOK FIFTY-EIGHT

"THE REDEDICATION OF NICKY"

**Sunday**          **12:30-1:00 p.m.**          **April 28, 1946**

*ANN:* One Man's Family, brought to you by the makers of Fleischmann's Yeast and Royal Desserts.

(ORGAN)

*ANN:* One Man's Family is dedicated to the Mothers and Fathers of the younger generation and to their bewildering offspring. Tonight we present Chapter Four, Book Fifty-eight entitled:

(ORGAN)

*ANN:* "The Rededication of Nicky"

(ORGAN)

*ANN:* For a very few days Nicholas Lacey has closed the Sky Ranch to everyone except his immediate family...That is his wife, Claudia; his step-daughter Joan and his own child Penelope. It's just as he explained to the family in Sea Cliff before he packed his own particular family unit in the car and drove away up the Sky Line:

*NICKY:* It's my opinion that a family is built on something vastly more significant than marriage ties or the fact that a child happens to be born to a certain father and mother. It's something that comes with close association; something each one contributes; something from the heart and personality of each member of the family. They somehow blend into a beautiful unit of society, and in each such unit a family lives, loves, feels safe and secure and above all, learns the four great humanities: self understanding; appreciation of his fellow mortals; realization of God; and, finally, something of the meaning of life and something of the reason he's put here. My family has almost disintegrated in the war years. I want some time alone with them up at the Sky Ranch while we reassemble our emotions and gather up the threads of human relations which have slipped from our fingers.

(ORGAN PICKS UP SOFTLY BEFORE ANN. BEGINS)

*ANN:* And so here are Nicholas Lacey back from a Japanese prison camp, and Claudia Barbour Lacey, likewise home from a war concentration camp, once more in their own suite of bedrooms on the second floor of the big old ranch house at the Sky Ranch. Joan isn't reconciled to her mother by a long way yet, but she DID allow Claudia to kiss her cool, unresponsive little cheek as she was tucked in her bed for the night. As for Penny, she said her prayers on her knees and then tumbled into bed with a moist kiss for both Nicky and Claudia and the next instant was deep in sleep. And now Claudia is in her bed and Nicholas, in bathrobe and slippers, stands looking down at her.

*CLAUD:* *(amused)* Well, aren't you at least going to sit here for a little?

*NICKY:* *(amused)* I say, I never thought to feel a stranger in my own house...

*CLAUD:* *(amused)* A stranger?

*NICKY:* *(agrees)* I didn't until the moment I came through the adjoining bath to your room...and suddenly I was seized with a most amazing confusion...

*CLAUD:* *(amused)* You mean you feel like a strange man in a strange lady's bedroom?

*NICKY:* *(amused)* I do for a fact...

*CLAUD:* *(gently)* Sit down here Nicky...

*NICKY:* *(amused)* Righto...At least I need no urging...

*CLAUD:* *(little laugh)* ...Now put this pillow behind your back...There! How's that?

*NICKY:* You're very proficient at putting a man at his ease...

CLAUD: *(amused) (agrees)* Uh huh, I always thought I'd make a good hostess... *(suddenly earnest)* Oh Nicky, Nicky, it's TRUE.

NICKY: *(agrees)* I don't quite believe it myself; but here we *are*.

CLAUD: *(whispers)* I...I get the shakes just looking at you...

NICKY: *(amused)* STILL?

CLAUD: Uh huh...

NICKY: I wonder if you had that strange sense of unreality when you first returned...All the old familiar things and places...A hair brush on the dresser just where I put it down four years ago...Slippers I took off when I went away so suddenly...so unexpectedly. The good, clean, out-of-doors smell to my room I've always liked so much...

CLAUD: It's been kept that way with loving hands, Nicky...Shortly after...after we were reported missing at sea, Clifford and Irene came up here...They kept this whole suite of rooms just as you and I left them...

NICKY: I suppose someone must have...The place would have become a deserted house full of must and decay in four years.

CLAUD: We owe Clifford more than you know...

NICKY: He's coming back up here to stay...

CLAUD: Oh good...he and Skippy?

NICKY: *(agrees)* By all means, Skippy...

CLAUD: Oh, I'm glad...When?

NICKY: Let's see...This is Saturday...They'll be here Wednesday or Thursday of next week...By the way, are you sleepy?

CLAUD: Oh NO, Nicky...

NICKY: Then I'd like to tell you about tomorrow...

CLAUD: Sunday?

NICKY: Yes...tomorrow afternoon...We're going down to the little church in Woodside.

CLAUD: Church...But Nicky, there's no church services in the afternoon.

NICKY: There is tomorrow...a special one...I've arranged it just for us...

CLAUD: You and me?

*NICKY:* And Joan and Penelope...The little white church sets back in the woods away from the road...When we go down there the windows of the church are going to be open and the organ playing...We'll walk about under the trees a little, listening to the music and then we'll find a spot of grass and make ourselves comfortable and the minister is coming out and talk to us.

*CLAUD:* *(uneasy)* But...But Nicky, I don't understand...

*NICKY:* My dear, I think it quite time we had a rededication of family ties; a repledging of faith in ourselves and each other.

*CLAUD:* *(fear)* You...You've found out about Gregory Lusk, haven't you?

*NICKY:* Yes, Claudia...

*CLAUD:* *(relief)* I'm glad...I'm glad it's out...

*NICKY:* So am I, if it's any relief to you...Otherwise it doesn't matter...As we pledged ourselves on the day I came home...we have buried the past. What is buried must be dead and what is dead cannot come back to hurt us...

*CLAUD:* *(uneasy)* Is...Is that why we're going down to the church tomorrow afternoon?

*NICKY:* Some small part perhaps...Just as the ugly rebellion in Joan is some small part...And my own misgivings and need for personal readjustment is some of it...Don't you understand, my dear; it's no one person or no one thing; it's simply that we're a family that has strayed and lost itself in the maelstrom of today's desperate living...And I think this is a way to help us return to what we had before.

*CLAUD:* I...I've never done anything like this...It...It seems strange...

*NICKY:* It's something I've wanted to do for a long time...I thought about it in the prison camp near Tokyo...I thought about it out there behind the enemy lines on the edge of India...The rededication of myself and my family to beauty and truth and honorableness...

*CLAUD:* Nicky, something happened to you out there...

*NICKY:* Quite...I suddenly realized that the world is being eaten up by greed and selfishness...Greed is like a parasite smothering a tree...It's RUST eating up iron ...Greed is eating the iron out of the soul of the world...

*CLAUD:* Something happened to you PERSONALLY...*(pause)* ...Something DID, didn't it?

*NICKY:* *(tense)* The past is buried...It's not good to dig up the bones of the dead!

(ORGAN SEGUE INTO SOFT ORGAN BACKGROUND)

*ANN:* And now it is Sunday afternoon outside the church in Woodside!

(RECORD OF MEADOWLARK OR BIRDS OF SIMILAR NATURE OFF AND ON IN BACKGROUND)

*PENNY:*   (*on cue*) Somebody's playing the organ in the church.

*NICKY:*   (*agrees*) Jolly, isn't it?

*JOAN:*   (*sullen*) Are we just going to walk around outside here under the trees?

*NICKY:*   For the moment, yes, Joan...

*PENNY:*   Would you like to take my hand, Claudia?

*CLAUD:*   (*subdued*) Yes, darling...

*PENNY:*   Would you like to take my OTHER hand, Nicky?

*NICKY:*   (*agreeable*) I would, indeed...And with my other hand I would like to hold one of yours, Joan...

*JOAN:*   (*shrugs*) If you want to...

*PENNY:*   I know what the organ's playing NOW, Claudia...

*CLAUD:*   Do you, Penny?

*PENNY:*   Yes, it's I Walked in the Garden. They played it in Sunday School when I went with Margaret...

*CLAUD:*   Did they?

*PENNY:*   Yes...Why are we walking around OUTSIDE the church...Why don't we go INSIDE?

*CLAUD:*   You'll have to ask your father that...

*PENNY:*   WHO?

*CLAUD:*   Nicky...He's your father...Have you forgotten?

*PENNY:*   (*laughs*) I guess I kinda DID...You've got to have a father quite a while before you remember him, I guess.

*NICKY:*   (*amused*) No apologies necessary...If a father doesn't stay put in a father's place, then he deserves to be forgotten...

*PENNY:*   But I LOVE you...

*NICKY:*   Quite...I'm very much in love myself this afternoon...In fact my heart is FULL of Joan and Claudia and you at the moment...

*JOAN:*   (*sullen*) But why DON'T we go inside?

*NICKY:* It's warm out here...It's gloriously quiet and peaceful. I thought perhaps we'd be closer to something listening to the music out here...In a moment, the Minister for this church is coming out here and talk to us...I thought it would be more informal, more intimate out here.

*PENNY:* Now the organ's playing something else!

*NICKY:* Yes...I say, he'll be along any moment now...Let's sit down on this grassy bank and listen to the music and wait for him. Claudia...?

*CLAUD:* *(subdued)* Yes, Nicky.

*NICKY:* *(little effort)* Righto...and here we are...

*JOAN:* *(low) (sullen)* I never heard of anything like THIS before...

*NICKY:* *(agrees)* Naturally not...There's never been a situation quite like this, I don't suppose...

*CLAUD:* *(low, nervous)* Here he comes, Nicky...

*NICKY:* Yes, I see him.

*PENNY:* I don't see him...

*NICKY:* Through the trees...Hush, now...

(LONG PAUSE WITH JUST MUSIC IN BACKGROUND)

*MINISTER:* *(on cue)* Good afternoon, all of you...God bless you. *(pause)* It's a little hard to know just how to begin this little service this afternoon. It's unique in my experience as well as in yours. I've looked forward to it with the deepest pleasure since I was asked to participate in it. Before me sit four of you...Four parts of a family...four parts of a broken family; and this afternoon we've come here to reunite...to rejoin...to rededicate the union which made this family possible in the beginning. One of you is only a few days home from the wars...two others of you are just emerging from the terrors of famine and filth and degradation of Europe...one of those two hardly more than a child in arms. The fourth member, a young girl of tender years, had perhaps the hardest vigil of all...It was she who was left behind...lonely...deserted...no one to call her own...no family ...no mother to understand her...no father to comfort her...

*JOAN:* *(begins to cry)*

*CLAUD:* *(near tears herself)* Joan, darling...No, darling...No, darling...*(softly)* ...There...there...there...

(LONG PAUSE WITH JUST MUSIC BEHIND)

*MINISTER:* *(on cue)* Lord, my heart is not haughty nor mine eyes lofty, neither do I exercise myself in great matters, or in things too high for me.

Surely I have behaved and quieted myself as a child that is weaned of his mother; my soul is even as a weaned child.

Let me hope in the Lord from henceforth and for ever.

(LONG PAUSE WITH JUST MUSIC BEHIND) (SEGUE TO MUSIC BEHIND WED-
DING CEREMONY)

*MINISTER:* *(on cue)* Nicholas Lacey, will you stand up, please...

*NICKY:* *(softly)* Quite.

(PAUSE)

*MINISTER:* *(on cue)* Claudia Barbour Lacey, will you rise and stand by his side.

*NICKY:* *(softly)* Give me your hand, my dear...

*CLAUD:* *(softly)* Yes...

(PAUSE)

*MINISTER:* *(on cue)* Nicholas and Claudia, for the last 40 months there has been
great turmoil in your lives and especially in your spirits. Thunder has rolled
through your souls and lightning has flashed there and a great rain of tears has
flooded the desolate places of your hearts. You were lost to one another, and
sometimes you were even lost from yourselves. Some of the evil which has
crept over the world in these days of hatred and defiance and lust; lust for
power...lust for gain...lust for all that is not part of man's finer being. Lust and
despair swept over the world, and some of the dust of this iniquity filtered into
the souls of men. And now today we are here to cleanse, to sweep out, to dust
away all that is not good and true and wholesome; so that those things which
were there are no longer there. The evil past is no more and what is no more
never was; only good survives! Therefore Claudia and Nicholas, I say unto you
this day you are made whole; the goodness of the past is linked with the goodness of the present, and your lives are one continued flow of joy in each other
from beginning to end, which is forever.

(PAUSE)

*MINISTER:* Joan, will you rise and stand between Claudia and Nicholas. *(pause)*
Will you take the hand of your mother...*(pause)* With your other hand, will you
take the hand of your father...

*JOAN:* *(whispers)* He isn't my father...

*MINISTER:* He is if you wish him to be...if you do take his hand...

(PAUSE)

*NICKY:* *(softly)* Good girl...

*MINISTER:* *(slight pause) (on cue)* Joan, this day your father and mother rededicate their love to you; they assure you of family security; of devotion and all else
that a child may expect from its parents, but mainly love. But in order to receive

love you must GIVE love. Will you open your heart to pour out the love which is there and to receive their great affection in return? Will you do this?

JOAN: *(uneasy)* I...I'll try.

MINISTER: To try sincerely is to succeed. *(slight pause)* Penelope...

PENNY: I was wondering if you were going to leave me out.

CLAUD: *(laughs, near tears)* Come on, darling...

MINISTER: No one is ever left out of the family circle...Having joined hands you are now a complete circle...A complete whole...A unit in God and in Society... May this family receive the blessing of God and forever feel the precious magnetism of love flowing from one heart to the other...*(Slight pause)* And now, repeat after me...

UNISON: *(After Minister has started alone)*
I will lift up mine eyes unto the hills, from whence cometh my help.
My help cometh from the Lord which made heaven and earth.
He will not suffer thy foot to be moved; he that keepeth thee will not slumber.
Behold, He that keepeth Israel shall neither slumber nor sleep.
The Lord is thy keeper; the Lord is thy shade upon thy right hand.
The sun shall not smite thee by day, nor the moon by night.
The Lord shall preserve thee from all evil; He shall preserve thy soul.
The Lord shall preserve thy going out and thy coming in from this time forth, and even for evermore.

(ORGAN)

ANN: You have just heard Chapter Four, Book Fifty-eight of One Man's Family, written and produced under the direction of Carlton E. Morse for the makers of Fleischmann's Yeast and Royal Gelatin.

# CHAPTER TEN

## "This I Give"
## Father Barbour's Legacy

Having ransacked the pigeonholes of my desk, emptied my drawers of 50 years of accumulations, and perused my daybooks, yearbooks, files, etc., kept meticulously since Fanny and I were married on the tenth day of May, 1896, I feel compelled to segregate from the accumulation some of the highlights—some sentimental, some humorous, some solemn, but all dear to me—and put them aside in an orderly manner for whatever usefulness and edification they may be to my family.

Inasmuch as this all has to do with my family specifically, and in a larger sense all American families, I choose to begin with an excerpt from a letter written to Claudia back in 1931 on the occasion of her elopement to Reno with Johnny Roberts, Joan's father:

> Marriage is the gateway through which a man or woman obtains great personal experience in the field of human relations. Parenthood is the opportunity for putting that experience to practical use. Parents should not in selfishness say, "We shall have children because it is our God-given right," but rather, "We shall have children because we are able to give them an intelligent physical, mental, moral and spiritual heritage. Mother love may be beautiful in itself, but mother love combined with understanding discipline is the force that turns the child into a happy, well-adjusted, mature man or woman and a good citizen. Neglected and misguided offspring result in one of civilization's most appalling wastes and expensive problems. For an undisciplined, unprincipled boy makes a heed-

less man, and a lazy, unmindful girl makes an indifferent woman, and both are useless citizens—another human life wasted, another burden for civilization to bear.

Good citizenship is prerequisite to an abundant and gracious civilization and thoughtful parenthood is the key to good citizenship. Great civilizations three times before have withered and died because they neglected this important truth.

This is the first and final purpose of family life, and it is my hope and intent that the contents of the following pages will bear me out.

One word further: if the remainder of the presentation appears to take the form of a holographic will or codicil, I wish to state that all my property, monies, and material things are provided for in a properly devised document resting in the safe deposit vaults in the law offices of Judge Glenn Hunter. What follows in the manner of bequeaths and bequests, etc. are the more precious and lasting matters that lie deep in my heart and in my mind after 57 years as husband and father and are in no way concerned with the law.

This, then, is the holographic will of Henry Barbour set down in March of 1953, devised for the simple purpose of conveying and bestowing upon my loved ones certain riches out of the fullness of my heart.


**This I Give...**

To my wife, Fanny, I give my infinite appreciation and love for her gentleness and goodness and devotion with which she has surrounded me and our home all our married life, and which blessed attributes she has implanted in each of our five sons and daughters. Because of this that she has done as good wife and mother, our nation has been strengthened and the world is a better place.

**This I Give...**

To my eldest son, Paul, I give my love and continued admiration for the fine and honorably, morally and intellectually mature man he has always been.

His code and conduct have been such that he has blessed his mother and father with pardonable pride. He has been an encouragement to his younger brothers and sisters and to my grandchildren, and no doubt this will continue for generations to come.

**This I Give...**

To my daughter, Hazel, I leave my special love for her unswerving devotion to her mother and me and to her husband and children. She has shone in the family firmament, a brilliant star of virtue, human understanding and generosity. Her "thinking" and her "doing" have added greatly to the meaning of personal and family integrity.

**This I Give...**

To my beloved son, Clifford, residing in foreign parts with a wife whom I have learned to love without knowing her, I give my most heartfelt prayers that goodness, happiness and love may always surround him and his. May he prosper, found a new dynasty and plant in this new place the seed of virtue that his mother bequeathed him.

**This I Give...**

To my beloved daughter Claudia, I bequeath the special care of Providence, who in its infinite wisdom knows so much better than human knowledge, how to comfort and quiet a restless spirit. May she come to know peace; may she finally find inner contentment; may God grant her in her physically mature years also maturity of mind, of emotions and of spirit; and may she and all that are closest to her be finally and happily blessed with peace and tranquility.

**This I Give...**

To my youngest son, Jack, I devise and bequeath a loving admiration and respect and the sure knowledge that by sheer dint of hard work and unswerving devotion to duty, and with eyes always fixed ahead on the horizon of truth, he will have not only more honest callouses, but more sturdiness of character, more love of the good, more final satisfaction, and more complete happiness, than any of my progeny. I love a sound, determined fighting man and I have him in my fifth offspring. Bless you, boy!

**This I Give...**

To my grandchildren, Joan and Penelope of Claudia's branch; Hank and Pinky and Margaret of Hazel's branch; Andrew of Clifford's branch; and Elizabeth Sharon Ann, Janie and Mary Lou *plus* the triplets, Abigail (Abbie), Deborah (Debby) and Constance (Connie) of Jack's branch—to all these, I bequeath a shining America of great and wonderful promise.

I give you a world that you, my grandchildren, with your physical, mental, moral and spiritual inheritance, can help to mold into the kind of a world you would wish for yourself and your progeny.

I bequeath you the never-ending task to so mold the world; I lay upon you the charge to *DO IT* and not turn your back upon it; I demand that you make this a better world by your own individual efforts; I urge upon you the need for ceaseless vigilance and implore you not to give away by barter, by appeasement, through ignorance, chicanery, indifference or in any other way, one inch of the free world, nor one word of free speech, nor allow to be closed one door of free worship.

To you I bequeath the burden and the joy of maintaining and enlarging our free world and the freedoms within our free world, which task is the most grueling and exacting but likewise the most worthy and honorable of any task ever laid upon any generation before you.

**This I Give...**

To my great-grandson, young Paul, scion of my granddaughter Joan and her fine husband, Ross Farnsworth, I give the whole world, which will in-

# A FATHER ON FATHER'S DAY

FATHER BARBOUR OF NBC's "ONE MAN'S FAMILY"

clude the year 2000! I give you the world that your mother and father's generation will have finally molded for you after I am long gone.

And may it be a world of goodness and happiness beyond the conception of man's mind in this muddled, befuddled age out of which we are straining to lift ourselves by our own bootstraps.

### This I Give...

And in conclusion, as I have introduced with my presence, the 20th century and my great-grandson in due course shall introduce with his presence the 21st, it is self-evident that this business of marriage and children and family life is a continuous and endless cycle, and no one is important save that in one manner or another he adds some small good that smoothes the way for those to follow.

And inasmuch as family life and the American way are here to stay far beyond the span of any one of us, it behooves us to make it the most perfect instrument of strength and goodness within our grasp and understanding. And that is what is in my heart to do and in the heart of each member of the Barbour family.

So with full heart and great thanksgiving for having been allowed a membership in this, the greatest of all human institutions, the American family, I sign my name on this 23rd day of the third month, in the year 1953.

*Father Barbour*

Editor's Note: *On the following pages we have reproduced certain pages from a premium booklet issued by one of the sponsors in 1953.*

# P R E F A C E

Having ransacked the pigeonholes of my desk, emptied
my drawers of fifty years of accumulations and perused
my day' books, year books, files, etc., kept meticulously
since Fanny and I were married on the Tenth day of
May, 1896, I have felt compelled to segregate from the
accumulation some of the highlights (some sentimental,
some humorous, some solemn, but all dear to me) and put
them aside in an orderly manner for whatever usefulness
and edification they may be to my family.

Inasmuch as this all has to do with my family specifically
and in a larger sense ALL AMERICAN FAMILIES, I
choose to begin with an excerpt from a letter written to
Claudia back in 1931 (May 7) on the occasion of her
elopement to Reno with Johnny Roberts (Joan's father).

"Marriage is the gateway through which a man or
woman obtains great personal experience in the field of
human relations. Parenthood is the opportunity for putting
that experience to practical use. Parents should not in
selfishness say, 'We shall have children because it is our
God-given right,' but rather, 'we shall have children

because we are able to give them an intelligent physical, mental, moral and spiritual heritage.'

"Mother love may be beautiful in itself, but Mother Love combined with understanding discipline is the force which turns the child into a happy, well-adjusted mature man or woman and a good citizen.

"Neglected and misguided offspring result in one of civilization's most appalling wastes and expensive problems. For an undisciplined, unprincipled boy makes a heedless man and a lazy, unmindful girl makes an indifferent woman and both are useless citizens . . . another human life wasted; another burden for civilization to bear.

"Good citizenship is prerequisite to an abundant and gracious civilization, and thoughtful parenthood is the only key to that good citizenship. Great Civilizations three times before have withered and died, because they neglected this important truth."

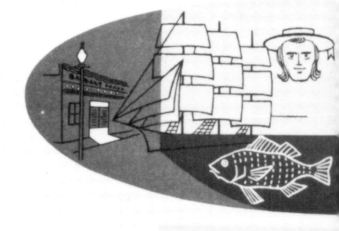

SAN FRANCISC

This then is the first purpose and the final purpose of Family life and it is my hope and intent that the content of the following pages will bear me out.

One word further, if the remainder of the book appears to take the form of a holographic will or codicil, I wish to state that all my property, monies and material things are provided for in a properly-devised document resting in the safe deposit vaults in the law offices of Judge Glenn Hunter. What follows in the manner of bequeaths and bequests, etc., are the more precious and lasting matters which lie deep in my heart and in my mind after fifty-seven years as husband and father and are in no way concerned with the law.

This then is the holographic will of Henry Barbour devised for the simple purpose of conveying and bestowing upon my loved ones certain riches out of the fullness of my heart.

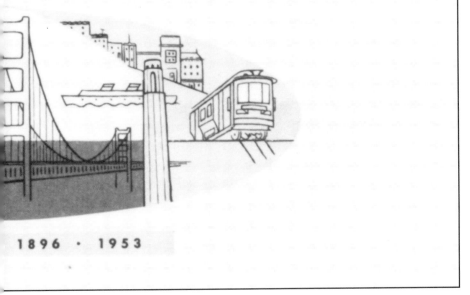

1896 · 1953

My favorite proverb for Fanny: "Where you have been I have been, and where I am you will come."

# This I give...

To my wife, Fanny, I give my infinite appreciation and love for her gentleness and goodness and devotion with which she has surrounded me and our home all our married life, and which blessed attributes she has implanted in each of our five sons and daughters. Because of this which she has done as good wife and mother, our own nation has been strengthened and the World is a better place.

anny's and my 20th anniver-
ary when we renewed our
ws before the Rev. Dr.
cArthur and congregation
llowing regular church serv-
es, November 14, 1916.

At old swimming hole first year Nicholas and
Claudia bought the Sky Ranch in 1934, before
renovation of house and addition of swimming pool. Fanny's hand has been in mine
always, down through the years.

# This I give...

To my eldest son, Paul, I give my
love and continued admiration
for the fine and honorable, and
morally and intellectually mature
man he has always been.
His code and conduct have been
such that he has blessed his
Mother and Father with pardonable
pride and has been an encouragemen
to his younger brothers and sisters
to my grandchildren, and no doub
will continue for generations to con

Teddy (l.) now veteran Army Nurse of World War II; West German Occupation; Japan Occupation and Korean War. She and her superior, Major Edith Aynes, were with us a few days at Christmas en route to their new post at HQ of 5th Army (Medical Section) in Chicago. Who could believe she is the little Teddy Lawton, Paul adopted 20 years ago.

Courtroom scene with judge the day Paul adopted Teddy July 10, 1933.

# This I give...

To my daughter, Hazel, I leave my special love for her unswerving devotion to her mother and me and to her husband and children. She has shone in the family firmament, a brilliant star of virtue, human understanding and generosity. Her "Thinking" and her "doing" have added greatly to the meaning of personal and family integrity.

Now this is what I call my ideal of a Second Generation. My daughter Hazel, and her husband Daniel are happy, home-loving parents in their own right. Hank is a senior at U. C., an all "A" student studying medicine. His twin brother, Pinky, is just finishing his service in the Navy at the Brooklyn Navy Yards and their sister, Margaret, is blossoming into a fine young lady. They are now living in the family home here because Fanny and I did so rattle around in this big house all by ourselves.

# This I give...

To my beloved son, Clifford, residing in foreign parts with a wife, Whom I have learned to love without knowing her, I give my most heartfelt prayers that goodness, happiness and love may always surround him and his May he prosper, found a new dynasty and plant in this new place the seed of virtue which his Mother bequeathed him.

No wonder Clifford is happy with his new wife, Mary, in Scotland. This is a recent picture he took of her and sent with several others. We are all charmed and do so hope to know her in person one day soon. In fact, if I was a few years younger I think I'd take Fanny and visit them.

# This I give...

To my beloved daughter, Claudia,
I bequeath the special care of
Providence, who in its infinite
wisdom knows so much better than
human knowledge, how to comfort
and quiet a restless spirit. May
she come to know peace; may she
finally find inner contentment;
may God grant her in her physically
mature years also maturity of mind,
of emotions and of spirit, and may
she and all that are close to her
be finally and happily blessed with
peace and tranquillity.

Editor's Note: *By 1953, Barbara Fuller had replaced Kathleen Wilson as Claudia.*

**My favorite proverb for Nicholas in reference to Claudia:** *Beauty adorns a man as candles a church.*

Nicky and Claudia represent the Barbours in Society and do it charmingly. This I believe was on the occasion of a Junior League Charity Ball.

# This I give...

To my youngest son, Jack, I devise and bequeath a loving admiration and respect and the sure knowledge that by sheer dint of hard work and unswerving devotion to duty, and with eyes always fixed ahead on the horizon of Truth, he will not only have more honest callouses, but more sturdiness of character, more love of the good, more final satisfaction and mo... complete happiness, than any of my pro... I love a sound, determined fighting man have him in my fifth offspring Bless yo...

Jack and Betty have just GOT to get a new family picture taken. The above, the only one I have dates back to 1950. They are holding the triplets and on the floor (l. to r.) are Janie, ten on May 15; Mary Lou, nine November 6 and Elizabeth Sharon Ann, eleven on June 9. Jack and Betty always refer to them as their six Beautiful Daughters.

They DO have this late one of the triplets, which I had taken myself. (l. to r.) Abagail, (Abbey) born ten minutes before midnight December 31, 1948; Deborah, (Debby) born exactly at midnight of the New Year and Constance, (Connie) born ten minutes into January 1, 1949.

*ny.*

*nd I*

*boy!*

# CHAPTER ELEVEN

## The Man of "The Family" Carlton E. Morse

**Carlton E. Morse** was born June 4, 1901 in Jennings, Louisiana. In 1906, at the age of five, he moved with his family to an alfalfa and dairy ranch in Jackson County, Oregon. He grew up on this ranch until the age of 17, when his family moved to Sacramento. After two years at the University of California, Morse left formal education to join the *Sacramento Union*.

After two years, Morse was taken on by the *San Francisco Chronicle* copy desk, and after several years was called to the *Seattle Times*. In Seattle he was given a human interest feature column, which he later brought back to San Francisco where he added the police beat to his growing knowledge.

Morse came to radio in 1929, pioneering radio drama and action shows, and learning which and what devices of radio held the public interest. It didn't take him long to discover the great feminine audience loved romance and the young people enjoyed mystery and adventure. Novelists had known this all along, but radio was a new media and nobody knew in those early days what the voice alone could do for entertainment. During the early days, Morse tried everything from the classic myths to falling-down comedy and, of course, mystery and adventure. It soon became apparent there was an audience for any type of drama so long as it was believable and well written.

In 1949, after 18 years as a half-hour radio show, "One Man's Family" was translated to the new medium of television. At the same time, the radio drama was changed to five 15-minute shows a week, and for the next nine years it was in two mediums at the same time. It was great fun! Who else, save the divine powers themselves and a scattering of novelists like Gertrude Stein and John Galsworthy, has had the experience of devising and maintaining a complete family universe satisfactory in every way to his pleasure and needs?

Morse says:

> "Do not think for one moment we are in any sense belittling the genius of the actors who played the various roles. Ineed, if it had not been for their capabilities, their loyalty and sincere affection for the Barbour family, none of my efforts would have borne fruit."

What has become of the principal actors of "The Family"? Let us take first those who are no longer with us.

Minetta Ellen, who for so many fans *was* Mother Barbour, died in 1965 at the age of 90 in Burbank, California. A serious case of pneumonia occasioned Minetta Ellen's sole absence from the show—a mere three broadcasts in 22 years. She retired from the show in 1955 at the age of 80.

J. Anthony Smythe, who created the role of Father Barbour and played in every show of the 27 years, died the same year as Mother Barbour at his home in Los Angeles. Ironically, one of the most famous fathers in radio was played by a bachelor. He played an amazing 1200 leading man roles on the stage in his 20 years with various companies before returning to California and moving to radio.

Barton Yarborough, who from the beginning was Clifford, died in 1951 of a heart attack in Hollywood. Like the other early cast members, he attended the University of California, acting in student productions. He later toured America in "Outward Bound," and acted in a London production of the same play. He was Joe Friday's original partner in both the radio and early television version of "Dragnet."

Of the remaining cast members, Michael Raffetto, who created the role of Paul, the eldest son, lives with is wife, Connie, in Berkeley, California. Bernice Berwin, the one and only Hazel through all the years, lives in the East Bay, near San Francisco. The actress who created the role of Claudia, Kathleen Wilson, is now Lady Kathleen Pilkington, wife of Lord Alastair Pilkington of London, England. She left the show to marry about the middle of its run and was replaced by Barbara Fuller. Finally, there is Page Gilman, who began the role of Jack when he was 12 years old, and remained with the cast until the show closed. He is retired now, and a full-time rancher in Oregon.

"These, then, are the principals who brought my dream family to life and gave it a breathing resemblance to the real thing in millions of American's hearts. I must not forget all those wonderful young people who played the third and fourth generation characters, or the husbands and wives of the principals. They, and occasional friends, were numerous. In fact, the chorus against which the principals laughed and danced and multiplied consisted of some 90 talented actors and actresses," Morse remembers.

"It is, I suppose, to be expected that with the end of "One Man's Family" on radio my relationship with the Barbour family is changed. It is as though the entire clan, the whole kit and kaboodle, had moved away from Sea Cliff Drive, San Francisco. Now, knowing little or nothing of their present activities, I no longer have much left but happy recollections of their adventures.

"Today I am absorbed in new creations. I have, in my mind, moved out of the world of the Barbour family and into a new neighborhood. My new acquaintances and new associations in my manuscripts are today's dear friends and completely absorb my creative interests. A dozen different Los Angeles families have come to life in my novel *Killer at the Wheel*, and a whole Montana valley of families and friends in a second novel *A Lavish of Sin*, both published in 1987. Oh yes, family affairs will always be a subject dear to my heart.

"But from this time forth, the Barbours of radio fame must live in the memories of all those millions who were so generously interested in the show. A public, you may be sure, that I will always hold in high esteem for its gracious and lasting loyalty."

---

## NBC AUTHOR TO BE FIRST ROUND
## TRIP PASSENGER ON CHINA CLIPPER

A lifetime of adventure will reach a new climax for Carlton E. Morse, NBC author, when he steps aboard the China Clipper April 28, as the first person in history to make a round-trip on a commercial trans-Pacific flight.

Hong Kong will be the destination as the twenty-five ton clipper roars over the Golden Gate; the other passengers will leave the ship there or at points en route, and even the crew will be changed at Honolulu on the return.

Already holder of the first ticket issued for the Pan American Airways flight, the author of the *One Man's Family* serial, also will receive the distinction of being the first person ever to travel to China and back in twelve days.

He will board the plane at Alameda, hop to Honolulu, make stops at the tiny Pacific Islands of Midway, Wake and Guam before reaching Manila, in the Philippine Islands.

The last stop before the Clipper arrives at Hong Kong will be the Portuguese Island of Macao, off the China coast.

As a former newspaper man, Morse has a high appreciation for "firsts" of any kind, and in this pioneering trip to the Orient he finds satisfaction of the reporter's yen for the dramatic. The quiet author of one of radio's most popular

CARLTON E. MORSE·
. . *reporter's yen for the dramatic*

serials believes it will top all thrills of a lifetime packed with action.

In the twelve days Morse will use in spanning the Pacific twice, he will miss only two of his coast-to-coast broadcasts of One Man's Family, now in it's sixth year. His scripts are written well in advance, and the job of producing the show, done by the author since its first days, probably will be handled by Michael Raffetto from suggestions Morse will leave behind.